╫

Lord, Open My Lips

╫

Lord, Open My Lips

The Liturgy of the Hours As Daily Prayer

Seth H. Murray

NORTH BAY BOOKS
EL SOBRANTE, CALIFORNIA

North Bay Books
P. O. Box 21234
El Sobrante, California 94820
(800) 870-3194
www.northbaybooks.com

Comments and inquiries regarding this book may also be sent to
john@northbaybooks.com

For quantity orders of this title for parishes and non-profit groups, please
contact the publisher.

All original material copyright © 2004 Seth H. Murray
Manufactured in the United States of America
Cover design by Elysium Design, San Francisco
Distributed by Publishers Group West.
ISBN: 0-9725200-8-2

Library of Congress Cataloging-in-Publication Data

Murray, Seth H. (Seth Hansen), 1970-
  Lord, open my lips : the Liturgy of the hours as daily prayer / Seth H.
Murray.— 1st ed.
     p. cm.
ISBN 0-9725200-8-2 (alk. paper)
1. Divine office. 2. Prayer—Christianity. I. Title.

BV199.D3M87 2004
264'.02015—dc22

                            2004018737

Contents

Preface

This book exists for selfish reasons, but not necessarily bad ones. Like you, I desire to be a good person: a good spouse, parent, friend, neighbor and businessman. All of these roles involve relationships that affect and are affected by each other, and especially by my relationship with Jesus. And so I desire to draw near to Jesus, to let him transform me and my relationships with others. This involves prayer. Yet try as I might, I have the hardest time bringing myself to do this seemingly simple act. There are always other pressing matters, most of them genuinely good and necessary. "I'll pray later" can gradually become "I'll pray never." Recognizing this tendency in my life, I suspected some years ago that healthy peer pressure might suffice in the absence of perfect charity, and so began my effort to organize what better people appear to do naturally: gather together to pray.

But pray how and what? All prayer, even the spontaneous kind, eventually becomes monotonous. If prayed to before each meal by every Christian, Jew and Muslim on the face of the earth, our poor Father in Heaven hears words to the effect of "God, thank you for this food" several billion times a day. An individual person expresses the same sentiment about 75,000 times during his life.

There is nothing wrong with habitual thankfulness — quite the opposite, in fact. But somewhere along the way questions must occur to most of us: "Why do I keep saying the same things over and over? What am I really doing?" Some try to make their prayers more eloquent and interesting, or implement methods to generate particular emotional states. But what really is the point of such activity? Is God somehow impressed by our mastery of language? Or is it only a kind of self-affirmation or comfort? "Ah, that was a good prayer."

Underlying such questions are more subtle ones: What is prayer? What is its purpose? Why pray at all? Thankfully, for the last 2,000 years the Catholic Church has practiced and promoted a form of Christ-centered prayer that is enriching and virtually inexhaustible. The contemporary version is called "the Liturgy of the Hours," and it answers most of these questions.

Having discovered what to pray, I then faced the task of learning how to pray it. Ideally, one would learn by visiting other prayer groups, but these are in short supply. The Church's "General Instruction of the Liturgy of the Hours" does not serve well as a standalone guide to learning to pray the Hours. And teachers, clear instructions, time and support systems are scarce. Hence this book.

Treasures were uncovered during the learning process, not the least of which is the significance of chant and song in prayer. Guidance on how to chant and the Church's modern view of chanted prayer are almost nonexistent, but chant plays a much more important role than is at first imagined, and so a very simplified introduction is included in here.

Although this book draws almost exclusively upon Catholic sources, *Lord, Open My Lips* lends itself readily to ecumenical groups. Christians who would not naturally refer to themselves as "Catholic" will find within the Liturgy of the Hours an authentically Christian and inspiring font of prayer.

I extend my thanks to the many individuals and organizations who offered comments towards improving this text, especially Tyra Murray, Bernadette Shonka, Arianne Mullis, Kent Puntenney and Loren Willbur. Bill Sockey of the St. Thomas More Center for Family Life contributed many helpful suggestions. And John Strohmeier at North Bay Books deserves thanks for his patient efforts and for sharing my vision of making this book as widely available as possible.

Best wishes in your — in our — effort to open our minds and hearts to Jesus.

Lord, Open My Lips

Introduction

> Pray at all times in the Spirit, with all prayer and supplication. To that end keep alert with all perseverance, making supplication for all the saints, and also for me, that utterance may be given me in opening my mouth boldly to proclaim the mystery of the gospel, for which I am an ambassador in chains; that I may declare it boldly, as I ought to speak. (Ephesians 6:18-20)

Christians are called to consecrate every moment of every day to God. Every action. Every thought. Every word. This is a tremendous and seemingly impossible task, but it is part of our gift and duty as a people who participate in Christ's priestly activity.

Those who attempt to live a life of prayer find it difficult. How quickly the mind is distracted. How quickly we find ourselves falling into monotonous patterns. How quickly we find that we simply don't know how or what to pray, and if we knew, we may not want to do it.

> In matters of prayer we are only too apt to deceive ourselves because, generally speaking, man does not enjoy praying. He easily experiences boredom, embarrassment, unwillingness, or even hostility. Everything else appears to him more attractive and more important. . . . [But without] prayer, faith becomes weak and the religious life atrophies. One cannot, in the long run, remain a Christian without praying, as one cannot live without breathing. (Msgr. Romano Guardini, *The Art of Prayer*)

But Christ, through the Church, helps us. Prayer is certainly more than informing God about what is going on in our lives — something He already knows. At its essence, prayer is a lifting, opening and offering of the heart and mind to God. For this the Liturgy of the Hours is an incomparable guide.

One could write volumes on what prayer is and how one engages in prayer. Different authors identify different elements, levels, types, expressions, intentions and fruits of prayer. It is not the intention of this text to provide such an education. Rather, we recommend reading the later sections of the *Catechism of the Catholic Church* (CCC) on prayer, especially paragraphs 2626-2643 on elements of prayer, and 2700-2719 on expressions of prayer. *The Art of Prayer*, by Romano Guardini, is also recommended. For the sake of this tutorial, we will allow the prayer itself to teach us as we pray it.

If you have never heard of the Liturgy of the Hours, don't be embarassed. Many who are very familiar with Catholicism and methods of prayer are not familiar with it. If they have not heard the term, they may have heard of some of its individual prayers. From the Latin: *Matins, Lauds*, *Vespers*, *Compline*, and so forth.

In fact, the Liturgy of the Hours is known by several relatively familiar names:

- The Liturgy of the Hours
- The Divine Office
- The Breviary (referring to the book)
- *Opus Dei* (the Work of God)
- Christian Prayer

To understand the meaning and importance of the Liturgy of the Hours, we must first understand the meaning of "liturgy." We can then move on to the substance of the prayers.

Liturgy . . .

Liturgy is an "action" of the whole Christ *(Christus totus)*. . . . It is the whole community, the Body of Christ united with its Head, that celebrates. Liturgical services are not private functions, but are celebrations of the Church, which is "the sacrament of unity," namely, the holy people united and organized under the authority of the bishops. Therefore, liturgical services pertain to the whole body of the Church. They manifest it, and have effects upon it." (CCC 1136-1140)

Liturgy is an action of the entire Church, responding to and acting under the influence of Christ's grace within her. It is distinct from popular piety or devotions, which are certainly graced, but not in the same way as a liturgical action. This is because liturgy is not merely an action of individual Christians, or even a group, but an action of Christ Himself. In liturgy, the people of God participate in and are caught up into the priestly, prophetic and kingly work of Christ in a way not otherwise accessible. Hence the Church's great emphasis upon increased understanding of and participation in liturgy.

. . . of the Hours

The Liturgy of the Hours is not a sacrament, but with the Liturgy of the Word, the Liturgy of the Eucharist, and the other liturgical actions, it is the Great Prayer of the Mystical Body of Christ, the Church. As such, it existed inchoate even prior to Christ's death and resurrection with the people God chose for Himself, the people known in various times and places as Hebrews, Israelites or Jews.

Among the earliest monotheistic traditions was that in which, two, three or more times per day, the people would individually or communally stop to offer prayer to God; morning, midday and evening. This tradition — a response to God's love and grace — continues uninterrupted to this day in Christianity as the Liturgy of the Hours.

From the *Catechism of the Catholic Church*:

1174 The mystery of Christ, his Incarnation and Passover, which we celebrate in the Eucharist especially at the Sunday assembly, permeates and transfigures the time of each day, through the celebration of the Liturgy of the Hours, "the divine office." This celebration, faithful to the apostolic exhortations to "pray constantly," is "so devised that the whole course of the day and night is made holy by the praise of God." In this "public prayer of the Church," the faithful (clergy, religious, and lay people) exercise the royal priesthood of the baptized. Celebrated in "the form approved" by the Church, the Liturgy of the Hours "is truly the voice of the Bride herself addressed to her Bridegroom." It is the very prayer which Christ himself together with his Body addresses to the Father.

1175 The Liturgy of the Hours is intended to become the prayer of the whole People of God. In it Christ himself "continues his priestly work through his Church." His members participate according to their own place in the Church and the circumstances of their lives: priests devoted to the pastoral ministry, because they are called to remain diligent in prayer and the service of the word; religious, by the charism of their consecrated lives; *all the faithful as much as possible*: "Pastors of souls should see to it that the principal hours, especially Vespers, are celebrated in common in church on Sundays and on the more solemn feasts. *The laity, too, are encouraged to recite the divine office, either with the priests, or among themselves, or even individually."* (Emphasis added, quoted from the Vatican II document, *Sacrosanctum Concilium, The Constitution on the Sacred Liturgy.*)

1176 The celebration of the Liturgy of the Hours demands not only harmonizing the voice with the praying heart, but also a deeper "understanding of the liturgy and of the Bible, especially of the Psalms."

1177 The hymns and litanies of the Liturgy of the Hours integrate the prayer of the Psalms into the age of the Church, expressing the symbolism of the time of day, the liturgical season, or the feast being celebrated. Moreover, the reading from the Word of God at each Hour (with the subsequent responses or *troparia*) and readings from the Fathers and spiritual masters at certain Hours, reveal more deeply the meaning of the mystery being celebrated, assist in understanding the Psalms, and prepare for silent prayer. The *lectio divina*, where the Word of God is so read and meditated that it becomes prayer, is thus rooted in the liturgical celebration.

1178 The Liturgy of the Hours, which is like an extension of the Eucharistic celebration, does not exclude but rather in a complementary way calls forth the various devotions of the People of God, especially adoration and worship of the Blessed Sacrament.

The Rosary Connection

The Liturgy of the Hours is the form of prayer from which the Catholic Rosary is derived. The Hours developed into its modern form around the traditional recitation of Psalms. In different times and places, illiteracy and other pressures made recitation of the Psalms difficult, if not impossible, especially among laity.

Consequently, while clergy and religious continued the traditional liturgy, workers in the field began to participate by reciting shorter, easier prayers while meditating upon the mysteries of the faith. Thus, rather than reciting 150 Psalms, a person praying a complete Rosary recites 150 "Hail Marys" while meditating upon various fundamental truths of the Christian faith. Although these shorter prayers — the Rosary, other chaplets, the Way of the Cross — are not liturgical but devotional in nature, they do maintain a connection to liturgy and sacraments. Hence, they are frequently called "sacramentals" or "para-liturgical prayers."

Praying the Liturgy of the Hours

Learning to pray the Liturgy of the Hours requires discipline. The books are big, and divided into poorly marked sections. The Church's "Instruction" was apparently written for people who already knew the prayers and don't need guidance. There aren't many teachers out there and, as with any act of prayer, an infinite number of other opportunities compete for one's time and attention. But as with many good things, the more difficult it is, the greater the reward for perseverance.

In this section we present a step-by-step outline, accessible to any lay person, for learning to pray the Divine Office.

1. Get a prayer book.
2. Get a supplementary guide book or calendar.
3. Familiarize yourself with the different sections of your book.
4. Learn the order of prayer.
5. Find a companion or teacher, if possible.
6. Make time to pray.

Step 1. Get a Prayer Book

There are several publications of the Liturgy of the Hours. It is important to choose the one that will be appropriate to your budget, temperament and available time. These are available through your local Catholic bookstore or various Internet book stores, and will set you back anywhere from $15 to $140, depending on which edition you choose. See the appendix for information for ordering these books.

If you intend to pray with a group, it will be helpful for you all to have the same version. There are minor differences between the same prayers in different books that can be confusing to beginners.

In addition, if everyone has the same books, it is easier to make sure everyone is on the right page.

THE COMPLETE LITURGY IN FOUR VOLUMES

If you are looking for a prayer book to last your entire life, this is the set to have. I encourage most people to use this edition. Each volume covers approximately one quarter of the year, so you can purchase them one at a time with a minimal impact on your bank account. It is, however, the most complicated set, and not recommended for anyone easily frustrated by book ribbons and page-flipping.

The largest sections of the complete set are "Office of Readings" and "Readings for Feasts, Memorials and Special Occasions." These are among the best resources available for learning Scripture and the writings of the saints and Church. If you would like to delve more deeply into Scripture and learn from the saints, this is the set for you. It is available in vinyl or leather-cover, and is published by Catholic Book Publishers.

THE SINGLE VOLUME

Some popular editions of the Liturgy of the Hours have been abridged to a single volume by the removal of most or all of "Office of Readings" and "Readings for Special Occasions." They are slightly easier to follow than the complete set, and some even include simple music/chant scores in the back for those wishing to learn to chant the Psalms. Publishers include Catholic Book Publishers and Liturgical Press.

SHORTER MORNING AND EVENING PRAYER

Also a single volume, the shorter prayer book has been pared down to only the Morning and Evening Prayers, although it sometimes includes Night Prayer, as well. This is a great starting point for those who want to learn the prayer, but aren't interested in the "Office of

Readings." It is also excellent for travel since it is so small. Some can just about fit into a large coat pocket. This version is available from several publishers.

ADAPTATIONS

Perhaps the best adaptation we've seen is produced by *Magnificat*. This is a monthly periodical that contains the entire Liturgy of the Mass, readings for each day, and abbreviated versions of Morning and Evening Prayer. Very easy to follow, it can be ordered directly from its publisher and is an excellent response to the Church's exhortation that the laity be encouraged to pray at least part of the Liturgy of the Hours. *Magnificat* is available by subscription, delivered directly to your home.

ONLINE RESOURCES

As of this printing there are two web sites that provide partial, online versions of the *Liturgy of the Hours* for personal and group use:

http://www.universalis.com/
http://www.liturgyhours.org/

SPECIAL NOTE FOR SHORTER EDITIONS

See the tutorial section for Morning Prayer if you have a condensed prayer book. It includes notes specific to smaller prayer books, and is easily adapted to evening and night prayer.

Step 2. Get a *St. Joseph Guide for the Liturgy of the Hours*

This is a paperback pamphlet, published annually, that costs about $2.00 and has the exact page numbers to which to turn on any given day of the year. Bookstores that carry the Liturgy of the Hours generally carry this supplement, as well. Be sure to get the *Guide* that goes with your particular book! There are different versions, some for the complete set and others for the single volume books. They are not interchangeable.

An alternative to the *St. Joseph Guide* is called the "Ordo." This pocket-size annual guide is commonly used by priests to determine daily Scripture readings and vestment colors, and gives brief summaries for the celebration of the Eucharist, along with the readings from the Liturgy of the Hours. However, it does not give specific page numbers, is not keyed to a particular edition, and is also a little cryptic until one becomes familiar with its acronyms.

A calendar that folds neatly into most any the Liturgy of the Hours prayer books is also available free online from the Apostolate of Prayer. (See resource list at the back of this book.) This calendar identifies the current week and any optional feasts one may wish to observe.

Once you are familiar with the prayers, calendars and supplements will rarely be needed.

Step 3. Familiarize Yourself with the Different Sections in the Prayer Book

Your prayer book is divided into sections, and once you become familiar with them you will have made great progress in practicing the Liturgy of the Hours. These sections are described below. Your edition may have more or fewer parts than are listed here. They are arranged differently in various books.

THE GENERAL INSTRUCTION OF THE LITURGY OF THE HOURS

This is included in its entirety at the beginning of volume one of the four-volume set. An abridged version is found in most others. The "General Instruction" is a fundamental document explaining the history, meaning, spirit and general practice of the Liturgy of the Hours. It has a great deal of good information, and is inspiring, but most people may find the "General Instruction" confusing or less than helpful in assisting them to actually learn how to pray the Divine Office in a step-by-step fashion. This is not due to any deficiency in the document. It was designed as a general text of supporting information about the Liturgy of the Hours, not a technical manual or tutorial.

THE ORDINARY

The Ordinary is a collection of outlines and directions for the prayers contained in your particular volume. It includes full texts of the most common recitations, especially the shorter prayers — openings and closings — that are shared by all of the individual "Hours." It is usually found towards the beginning of the smaller volumes and in the middle of the larger ones, right after the Proper of the Seasons. Read through it, get familiar with it, understand it, place a bookmark in it. Any time you get lost, which won't be uncommon when starting out, simply turn to the ordinary to find out what is next.

THE PSALTER

The Psalter, the core of the Divine Office, will be near the middle or in the front of your book. Sometimes the pages are marked with red edges to make them easier to find. At the top of every page is a heading such as "Week I," "Week II," etc.

It contains introductory text, hymns, Psalms, Canticles and prayers in a four-week cycle. Your volume will contain the material for at least the Morning and Evening Prayer. More complete volumes will also contain parts for the Office of Readings and Daytime Prayer.

THE PROPER OF THE SEASONS

This contains hymns, antiphons, Scripture readings and prayers unique to specific days and seasons. The complete Proper is found only in the four-volume set, the bulk of which is the Office of Readings, but a condensed version is in the single volume, and a highly distilled version is in some shorter prayer books.

NIGHT PRAYER

Even the shorter Christian Prayer books contain a few Night Prayers (also known as "Compline"). Night Prayer has a one-week cycle rather than a four-week-cycle, and is similar to the other prayers, but shorter.

THE PROPER OF SAINTS

Like the Proper of the Seasons, this section is found only in the comprehensive volumes. The Proper of the Saints and the Proper of the Seasons complement each other, but can be a source of confusion. The Proper of Saints contains alternative readings, usually the second reading for the Office of Readings, associated with a particular feast, solemnity or memorial day in the Church's calendar.

THE COMMONS

Usually found near the back of larger prayer books, it is closely related to the Proper of Saints. Many places in the Proper of Saints refer readers to the Commons, which contains prayers and readings shared "in common" by different feast days.

OTHER STUFF

Additional supplementary materials are found in the larger volumes. These contain alternative Psalms, readings, poems, and prayers.

Step 4. Learn the Order of Prayer

This will take a little time. Prayer requires effort, and the Liturgy of the Hours requires more than most. Now you have your book, but probably can't tell where to start. Don't worry! There is a general form common to all of the prayers.

GENERAL OUTLINE

All of the individual "Hours" follow a similar pattern, but some have longer parts than others. Though there are sometimes strict instructions for religious who pray the Divine Office, a general rule for laity is, "Do what you can." Certainly don't try to memorize all of this. It is tempting for the beginner to attempt too much and quickly get frustrated. Remember, you are under no obligation to pray the Liturgy of the Hours in its entirety, or follow this sequence of steps exactly.

- Introductory Prayers
- Hymn
- Psalms and Canticles with their Antiphons
- Scripture Reading
- Responsories
- Gospel Canticle
- Intercessory Prayers
- Concluding Prayer and Blessing

Once you've gone through the following tutorials, you should have a good feel for the overall flow of the Liturgy of the Hours. Here are some important keys to successfully praying the Divine Office:

1. Get to know the Ordinary. The Ordinary is your friend.
2. The labels don't always mean what they mean (e.g., Sunday Evening Prayer I). This will make sense later.
3. Do not recite red print, headings, reflective or instructional text.
4. A lot of the Liturgy is optional. For laity, it's all optional. Focus on those parts that are interesting to you and grow from there. Don't feel bad for praying only one prayer, or even just part of one.
5. Be aware of "liturgical shorthand." Many entries in the prayer books are only the first few words of larger prayers.

6. Be aware of "invisible prayers." These are prayers that are customarily prayed at certain points, but don't always show up in the instructions (e.g., "Glory Be . . ." after every Psalm or Canticle).

7. Be sure to make good use of ribbons or bookmarks. This comes with practice.

8. Don't worry if you get lost. It is better to pray the Liturgy poorly than not at all, and it soon gets easier and becomes intuitive.

Step 5. Find a Teacher or Prayer Companion

Although it is perfectly permissible to pray the Divine Office in private, and private prayer is immensely better than none at all, it is ideally suited and intended to be prayed with others.

A teacher can be difficult to find, and even more so if you need to find one who can meet outside of normal work hours. It is among the responsibilities of your parish priest to make himself available to teach and lead the Liturgy of the Hours, but many are too busy. Consider yourself very fortunate if your priest is able to work with you on this.

You can also contact local convents or monasteries. They frequently welcome guests and are eager to teach this form of prayer. Further, they generally pray the complete Liturgy of the Hours every day, so you'll have a choice of times at which to join them. One word of warning: Some religious orders pray their own unique Psalter (group of Psalms). This may be confusing if you are trying to learn to pray from the standard English books.

If you can't find a teacher, try to find someone who will learn with you. If you are committed to praying with someone else, it will help both of you to continue.

Step 6. Make Time to Pray

Distractions will readily present themselves, especially at the beginning, but try to establish a routine of specific times for prayer in your daily schedule — first thing in the morning, before a meal, before retiring at night. Jesus exemplifies for us the importance of making time for prayer. He regularly retired to places away from the public eye to pray to his heavenly Father. Find a quiet room. Close the door. Turn off the pager and the cell-phone. Gather yourself, alone or with companions, into prayer without disruptions.

Start modestly, making it your goal not to pray as much as you possibly can, but as much as you should and as is appropriate to your place in life.

An effective way of bringing structure into your prayer life is to find a lay organization at your workplace or in your area that regularly prays together. A later chapter offers guidance for starting a prayer group if one is not available.

The Calendar of the Liturgy of the Hours

Knowing what to pray on what days can be confusing at first. One solution is to get an inexpensive Liturgy of the Hours guide or calendar (see page 18). It will save you from worrying about where to turn and what to pray, because it lists the exact page numbers to go to for every day of the year. But if you don't have a guide — and even if you do — it is helpful to know the basic rules for finding the correct week in the Psalter:

Week I begins on the following days. Count the weeks from these dates to get to the proper week and day.

- First Sunday of Advent
- Monday after the Baptism of the Lord
- First Sunday of Lent
- Easter Sunday

Knowing which prayers to pray in the Proper of Seasons and Proper of Saints is a little more straightforward (no higher math skills are required). For the Proper of Seasons, simply locate the appropriate week or season. If it is the 18th week of Ordinary Time, use that section of the Proper. If it is November 30, the Feast of the Apostle Andrew, substitute those parts found in the Proper of Saints. If it is December 1, for which there is no entry in the Proper of Saints, remain in the Psalter and Proper of Seasons.

If this is confusing — and it is for most people at first — just use the regular Psalter and Proper of Seasons until you are familiar enough with the Liturgy to start using the Proper of Saints.

Once you begin praying with regularity, keeping track of where to begin becomes much easier. Leave your ribbons at the pages where you end, then pick up at that point the next time you use your prayer book. More details on observing memorials, feasts and solemnities are in a later chapter.

Frequently Asked Questions

HOW MUCH SHOULD I TRY TO PRAY AT ONCE?

Only as much as you have time for, but do make time every day to try at least one of the prayers, preferably Morning or Evening Prayer.

WHY ARE THERE TWO DIFFERENT SUNDAY EVENING PRAYERS IN MY PRAYER BOOK?

Sunday Evening Prayer I is for Saturday evening. Sunday Evening Prayer II is for Sunday evening. Why? According to tradition, "tomorrow" begins at sundown, today. (Have you ever wondered why you can go to Mass on Saturday evening and have it "count" as a Sunday Mass? Now you know.)

WHERE CAN I LEARN MORE?

Check to see if a parish in your area has a group that prays the Liturgy of the Hours (sometimes offered under the names "Lauds," Vespers" or "Compline"). Another good place to start is the nearest convent or monastery. They pray the Divine Office in its entirety and most are happy to share it with you. You might also try arranging an appointment with your parish priest or deacon for instruction.

WHERE CAN I GET PRAYER BOOKS?

You can find them at your local Catholic bookstore, at some general bookstores, or through sources on the Internet. See the Appendix for editions and publishers.

WHICH IS THE RIGHT PRAYER BOOK FOR ME?

Unless cost prevents you, we strongly recommend the four-volume set, *The Liturgy of the Hours*. One of the greater needs in today's

Church is a renewed understanding of the faith by the laity. A superb resource for this is Scripture and prayer, of course, but also the interpretation and application of Scripture as found in the Office of Readings. Smaller volumes either truncate the Office of Readings, or eliminate it altogether.

If the cost of the larger set is prohibitive, you can purchase just the volume for the present season. By spreading the cost out in this way, you'll spend around $10 a month and have the entire set within a year. With a little searching, it is also possible to find used copies in good shape. An investment in the complete version will repay you throughout your lifetime.

For those who travel frequently, *Shorter Christian Prayer* is convenient due to its size. The larger, single volume *Christian Prayer* is nice, too, but it is the same size as any single book from the four-volume set, and so doesn't do much for convenience.

Lord, Open My Lips has been tested and edited to serve as a guide no matter which edition you select. Although based primarily on the four-volume set, which alone includes the full text of the Liturgy of the Hours, it will adapt easily to shorter versions.

CAN MUSIC BESIDES CHANT BE USED WITH THE LITURGY OF THE HOURS?

Yes. It is important, however, that the music selections not distract one from the prayers themselves. The music should harmonize with the prayers and help you to lift and open your mind to God. If it isn't doing this, then it may be better to use a different form of music or have no music at all.

WHICH PARTS OF THE PRAYERS CAN BE CHANTED?

The entire prayer may be chanted, but it is most common to chant or sing only the Psalms and Canticles. However, one isn't required to chant or sing any part.

WHY IS THE **"G**LORY **B**E**" (D**OXOLOGY**)** DIFFERENT THAN THE ONE **I** KNOW**?**

Lord, Open My Lips uses the exact language of the revised Liturgy of the Hours. If you prefer, or if you are part of a group that prays the more traditional Doxology, feel free to do so.

MY PRAYER BOOK HAS **[1,2,3,4,5]** RIBBONS. **W**HERE DO **I** PUT THESE**?**

Please see the next section.

Setting Up Your Prayer Book

Ribbons

Almost every version of the Liturgy of the Hours shares one thing in common: ribbons. Depending on which book you have, you might see anywhere from one to five ribbons popping out of the top.

Some ribbons are not attached to the binding, but to a plastic card that is inserted into the spine. With use, the ribbons are the first items to wear out. Because they are not bound in, you can replace them easily without replacing the whole book.

ONE-RIBBON BOOKS

Some shortened prayer books will have one ribbon. Place this ribbon in the Psalter.

TWO-RIBBON BOOKS

Books with two ribbons usually have two distinct sections; a Psalter and the Readings. Place one ribbon in each area.

FIVE-RIBBON BOOKS

Okay, here we go! Place one ribbon at the beginning of each of the following sections. You'll move them to the correct page as you go through the tutorials:

- Proper of the Seasons
- Ordinary
- Psalter
- Night Prayer
- Proper of the Saints

Don't have any ribbons? Lost them? Holy cards or regular book-marks are good substitutes.

As you finish each prayer, simply move the ribbons ahead to the beginning of the prayer for the following day. If you get into the habit of doing this (and don't miss too many days in a row), then it becomes fairly easy to stay on track with the right prayers for a given day.

Sticky Help

Common prayers like the Canticle of Zechariah or Canticle of Mary — the Gospel Canticles — are in the Ordinary. Some prayer books come with additional cards with these and other common prayers on them. It can be helpful to keep these cards tucked into the front or back cover of your prayer book for easy locating. Some people paste the Gospel Canticles inside the covers using rubber cement. You will soon understand why that is a good idea.

Using The Tutorials

Books

Lord, Open My Lips is drawn primarily from volume I of the complete four-volume set of the Liturgy of the Hours, although notes are included for other editions, particularly in the tutorial for Morning Prayer. Volume I is usually blue, and covers Advent and Christmas. It is easier to begin and learn the order of prayer in an Ordinary Time volume (volume III or IV) or the Ordinary Time section in an abridged version (which can almost be prayed "straight through"), but we are starting here because volume I includes an "average" amount of flipping from one area to another within the book.

Day of the Year

The following tutorials use the First Monday of Advent as the example for all prayers.

Fonts

For the sake of clarity, we have tried to make the excerpts from the Liturgy of the Hours resemble the actual text in your prayer book. In general, headings and any words in red, grey or italics in your prayer book are not said aloud. The only words that are prayed out loud appear in this font:

Times New Roman

Sequences and Optional Parts

Unlike the Sacred Liturgy of the Mass in which nearly every action and posture are carefully defined, the Liturgy of the Hours has relatively few "rubrics," and laity in particular are free and encouraged to adapt the Liturgy of the Hours to their particular needs (within reason). Those parts that are generally considered optional are noted as such in the tutorials, and marked with an asterisk (*) in the prayer outlines at the beginning of each tutorial.

Bear in mind that not all groups (or geographical regions) pray the Liturgy of the Hours in the same way. Some religious orders use a different Psalm sequence. Some groups add small parts or prayers, or might suppress others. Some say the antiphon twice at the beginning and once at the end. Some say it once at the beginning and omit it at the end. Some sing and chant. Finally, the order in which the individual prayers are listed is not necessarily the order in which they are prayed by all.

This can cause confusion, and it did so even in the development of this text. For the most part, however, the order of the prayers can be determined by a careful and thorough reading of the "General Instruction of the Liturgy of the Hours." Still some parts, especially optional or supplemental ones, remain ambiguous. For example, some publications of the American English edition of the Liturgy of the Hours include an optional Psalm-prayer in the text right before the final repetition of Psalm antiphons. In early editions of this text we directed people to pray the final verse of the Psalm, the Psalm-prayer, the Doxology, and then the final antiphon. Then the following excerpt from *From Breviary to Liturgy of the Hours: Structural Reform of the Roman Office, 1964-1971* was brought to our attention:

> It was clearly the mind of Group 9 that the Psalm prayer occur *after* the antiphon (if used) and pause for silent prayer, and not before the antiphon, as is the case in [the US Liturgy of the Hours]. The antiphon, said the canon, may be considered as almost part of the Psalm, and it is erroneous to place it after the Psalm prayer. (Footnote #300 from Chapter 5)

The contributor went on to argue that the position of the Psalm-prayer in the American English edition was an editorial decision of

Catholic Book Publishing Company. This is confirmed by the "General Instruction" in paragraph 202, where it explicitly refers to the Psalm-prayer as coming after the final antiphon for a psalm. Consequently, we changed the tutorials to reflect this.

However, the reader should be wary of becoming overly scrupulous regarding every posture, phrase and sequence. When visiting other groups, one is likely to encounter variation, and charitable liberty is important in such matters.

Leader

The tutorial assumes that only laity — one or more — will be present for the prayer. If a priest or deacon is present, it is normative for him to lead the people in prayer and give the final blessing. In the absence of clergy, any prepared lay person may do so.

Chanting

Chant is a moving and important part of the Liturgy of the Hours. However, it is also a topic unto itself, so a simplified introductory tutorial on chant is included near this book's end. Learn the basics first, then learn chant.

Sacred Silence

It is appropriate to have times of reflective silence throughout the prayers. Traditionally, these occur after the final antiphons of psalms, after readings, and before or after the Responsory. In private prayer there is more flexibility in these matters. In group prayer, such silences should not be so long, many or rigid as to distract from their purpose, which is to meditate upon the voice of God speaking to us through the prayers.

The Tutorials

INVITATORY ORDER

Stand

✠ "Lord, open my lips . . ."

Antiphon

Psalm 95 (or 100, 67 or 24)

Doxology

Antiphon

Proceed to Office of Readings or Morning Prayer

Invitatory Tutorial

The Invitatory precedes the Office of Readings or Morning Prayer, whichever you pray first in the day. The Invitatory is recommended, but sometimes omitted in private recitation by laity.

The bulk of the Invitatory is in the Ordinary, but the correct antiphon is sometimes found in the Psalter. It is a good habit to always turn to the Psalter first. Go ahead and do so now.

How is it prayed?

For this example, find the beginning of the section Monday, Week I, Invitatory in your Psalter. We will assume that it is the First Monday of Advent. It will begin:

MONDAY, WEEK I

Invitatory

Lord, open my lips.

Antiphon, as in the Ordinary, 647.

Invitatory Psalm, 648.

This is not the full text. It serves only as a reminder. The full text is in the Ordinary. Turn there now, keeping a finger (or ribbon) on Monday, Week I, Invitatory.

Stand, and while making the sign of the cross over your lips, say:

> Lord, open my lips.
> — And my mouth will proclaim your praise.

If there are two or more of you praying together, then one could pray the first line, while the other prays the second.

Next find the antiphon for the Invitatory Psalm (but don't pray it yet). These vary from season to season. An antiphon is usually a short phrase or sentence that acts as a brief refrain throughout a Psalm.

Notice that the Psalter stated, "Antiphon, as in the Ordinary." Sometimes the Invitatory Antiphon will be listed right in the Psalter, but in this case we are directed to find it in the Ordinary, where we read that the antiphon for the days between the First Sunday of Advent and December 16 is:

> Come, let us worship the Lord, the King who is to come.

Now that you've found the right antiphon, look for the Invitatory Psalm, usually Psalm 95, on the same or following page.

Psalm 95

A call to praise God

Encourage each other daily while it is still today
(Hebrews 3:13)

(The antiphon is recited and then repeated)

Come, let us sing to the Lord
and shout with joy to the Rock who saves us.

Let us approach him with praise and thanksgiving
and sing joyful songs to the Lord.

(Antiphon repeated)

. . .

There is some text in italics before the Psalm, a passage from Hebrews. Do not say this aloud. Merely reflect upon it for a moment.

Now say the antiphon. The Invitatory antiphon is typically said before the Psalm, between verses as noted in your book, and again after the Doxology, below. If you are praying as part of a group, it is common for the leader to recite the antiphon once, have it repeated by the group, and then begin the first verse of the Psalm. Groups vary on whether or not to repeat the antiphon between each verse, but it is common to do so between each verse of the Invitatory Psalm, or as noted in your particular book.

Psalm 95 is said, while standing, with its antiphon (other Psalms, such as 100, 67 or 24 are sometimes substituted, especially if Psalm 95 appears in later prayers for the day).

After finishing the Psalm, pray the Doxology.

> Glory to the Father, and to the Son, and to the Holy
>   Spirit:
> as it was in the beginning, is now, and will be for ever.
>   Amen.

Repeat the antiphon one last time. This concludes the Invitatory. If you have a ribbon in the Ordinary, this is a good time to make sure it is moved to the beginning of the next prayer you plan to pray (in the Ordinary), and then proceed to the Office of Readings or Morning Prayer.

OFFICE OF READINGS ORDER

Stand

Invitatory, or ☩ "God, come to my assistance . . ."

Hymn*

Sit

First Antiphon, Psalm and Doxology

First Antiphon*, Silence* and Psalm-Prayer*

Second Antiphon, Psalm and Doxology

Second Antiphon*, Silence* and Psalm-Prayer*

Third Antiphon, Psalm and Doxology

Third Antiphon*, Silence* and Psalm-Prayer*

Transitional Verse

Scripture Reading

Responsory*

Document Reading

Responsory*

Stand

Canticle, or Te Deum (Sundays, Feasts and Solemnities)

Concluding Prayer and Acclamation

Office of Readings Tutorial

The Office of Readings may be prayed at any time of the day. It is customarily prayed in the early morning, and will take fifteen to thirty minutes to complete.

The complete Office of Readings is found only in the larger editions. The bulk of the Office is in the Proper of the Seasons. There is an abridged Office of Readings in the large, single-volume *Christian Prayer* book. It follows the same principles, but in a four-week cycle. As with the other tutorials, turn first to the Psalter.

Introductory Prayers

For this example, find the beginning of the section Monday, Week I, Office of Readings in the Psalter of your prayer book. We will assume that it is the First Monday of Advent. If you have just prayed the Invitatory, skip the introductory prayers and go immediately to the hymn (next page). Otherwise, turn to the section for the Invitatory, or begin with the words "God, come to my assistance. . . ."

MONDAY, WEEK I

Invitatory

Lord, open my lips.

Antiphon, as in the Ordinary, 647.

Invitatory Psalm, 648.

Office of Readings

God, come to my assistance. Glory to the Father. As it was in the beginning. Alleluia.

This verse and response are omitted when the hour begins with the Invitatory.

This is not the full text. It serves only as a reminder. The full text is in the Ordinary. Turn there now, keeping a finger (or a ribbon) in the Psalter on Monday, Week I, Office of Readings. While standing, make the sign of the cross and pray:

Office of Readings

God, come to my assistance.
—Lord, make haste to help me.

Glory to the Father, and to the Son, and to the Holy
　Spirit:
as it was in the beginning, is now, and will be forever.
　Amen.

If there are two or more of you praying together, then one could pray the first line, the other prays the second, and so on.

The "Alleluia," noted in the Psalter but not in the Ordinary, is omitted during Lent.

Hymn (Optional)

Turning back to the Psalter, the listed hymn begins:

> O God of truth, prepare . . .

The hymn is entirely optional. It may be sung, chanted, read, substituted or omitted altogether. Sometimes the hymn won't be listed directly, or optional ones will be listed. When included, it is usually sung standing.

Psalmody

Psalmody

Ant. 1   Show me your mercy, Lord, and keep me
safe.

Psalm 6

A suffering man cries to God for mercy

*I am filled with dismay . . . Father, save me from this
hour* (John 12:27).

Lord, do not reprove me in your anger;
punish me not in your rage. . .

Be seated for the Psalmody, which consists of three Psalms (or parts thereof), along with their associated antiphons. For the First Monday of Advent the antiphon is (go ahead and recite it now):

Show me your mercy, Lord, and keep me safe.

Then follows the Psalm number, an editorial heading, and some text in italics before the actual Psalm. Do not say these aloud. Merely reflect upon them for a moment. When the Office is said (and not sung or chanted) some groups prefer to pray the text in black italics in place of the antiphon.

Psalm 6 is then said while seated. If praying with others, it is common to alternate reading/chanting individual verses, lines or entire paragraphs.

It might not be listed in your book, but unless noted otherwise, the Doxology is recited after *every* Psalm and Canticle:

Glory to the Father, and to the Son, and to the Holy
Spirit:
as it was in the beginning, is now, and will be for ever.
Amen.

Many books will show an optional Psalm-prayer immediately following some of the Psalms. However, this does not appear to be the intended order of Liturgy of the Hours. Rather, after the Doxology, repeat the antiphon for the first Psalm a final time, observe a brief moment of reflective silence, *then* pray the Psalm-prayer, if one is given. Then proceed to the next antiphon.

Psalm-prayer

Lord God, you love mercy and tenderness; you give life and overcome death. Look upon the many wounds of your Church; restore it to health by your risen Son, so that it may sing a new song in your praise.

Ant.   Show me your mercy, Lord, and keep me safe.

Repeat the above pattern two more times — antiphon, Psalm, Doxology, antiphon — with the appropriate Psalms, antiphons and Psalm-prayers as found in your prayer book, then note the instruction that reads

Verse, reading and prayer, as in the Proper of the Seasons.

This is instructing you to turn to the Proper of the Season to continue with the Office of Readings. It is where we will find the Verse. Be sure to leave the ribbon or bookmark where you are leaving off (or move it ahead to the beginning of your next intended prayer) in the Psalter.

Verse

The Verse acts as a transitional prayer between the Psalmody and the Readings. It is found in the Proper of the Seasons. Turn now to the beginning of your volume. Look for the page headings for the First Week of Advent, and then find Monday, Office of Readings. Immediately below this heading will be the Verse.

MONDAY

Office of Readings

Lord, show us your mercy and love.
— And grant us your salvation.

FIRST READING

From the book of the prophet Isaiah 1:21-27; 2:1-5

The judgement and deliverance of Zion. The gathering of the nations.

How has she turned adulteress,
   the faithful city, so upright!
Justice used to lodge within her,
   but now, murderers.

. . .

The verse, which begins, "Lord, show us your mercy . . ." is read aloud.

Readings and Responses

The readings in the Office of Readings are *long*. In private recitation, they are sometimes read silently and meditatively. In communal recitation, they may be read by a lector, or antiphonally as with the Psalms (alternating between readers).

The reading for the First Monday of Advent begins by saying:

From the book of the prophet Isaiah.

There follows some italic text in red. This is not read aloud, but merely summarizes the reading. Proceed to the reading.

It is common to have a short time of silence following the reading. The Responsory is sometimes omitted or adapted in private recitation. If you choose to say the Responsory, or are praying in a group then say:

RESPONSORY   MICAH 4:2; JOHN 4:25

Come, let us go up to the mountain of the Lord, to the
house of the God of Jacob.
— He will teach us his ways, and we will walk in his
paths.

The Messiah, who is called the Christ, is coming.
When he comes, he will teach us everything.
— He will teach us his ways, and we will walk in his
paths.

As with other similarly structured prayers, this can be prayed
antiphonally.

Repeat the above instructions for the Second Reading, which
is typically from the history of the Church or the writing of a saint.

Te Deum

Were this a Sunday, feast or solemnity, you would now stand and
say, sing or chant the Te Deum, found in the Ordinary. Otherwise,
proceed to the Concluding Prayer.

Concluding Prayer

Now you might find an enigmatic text that reads

Prayer, as in Morning Prayer.

This means that concluding prayer for the Office of Readings is
found at the end of Morning Prayer, right after the second reading
(probably one or two pages past your present place in the prayer
book). While standing, begin by saying:

Let us pray . . .

On this day the prayer is:

Prayer

Lord our God,
help us to prepare
for the coming of Christ your Son.
May he find us waiting,
eager in joyful prayer.

We ask this through our Lord Jesus Christ, your Son,
who lives and reigns with you and the Holy Spirit, one
God, for ever and ever.

Amen.

When celebrated communally, a final acclamation is added (found in the Ordinary):

Let us praise the Lord.
— And give him thanks.

This concludes the Office of Readings. Move your ribbon to the beginning of the next prayer for the day — probably on the same or following page — or the next prayer you intend to pray.

MORNING PRAYER ORDER

Stand

Invitatory or ☩ "God, come to my assistance . . ."

Hymn*

Sit

First Antiphon, Psalm and Doxology

First Antiphon*, Silence* and Psalm-Prayer*

Second Antiphon, Old Testament Canticle and Doxology

Second Antiphon*, Silence*

Third Antiphon, Psalm and Doxology

Third Antiphon*, Silence* and Psalm-Prayer*

Scripture Reading

Silence* and Message*

Responsory*

Stand

☩ Antiphon, Canticle of Zechariah and Doxology

Canticle Antiphon*

Intercessions

Our Father

Concluding Prayer and ☩ Blessing

Morning Prayer Tutorial

(This tutorial section, although based on the four-volume prayer book, includes notes for one-volume editions. If you have a one-volume prayer book, make similar adaptations for Evening and Night Prayer.)

Morning Prayer is prayed in the morning, usually sometime between 7:00 and 9:00AM. It is found, almost in its entirety, in the Psalter. (During special seasons, feasts, memorials or the like, the second half of the prayer is in the Proper of the Seasons, the Proper of Saints, or the Common.) Turn to your Psalter now.

Introductory Prayers

For this example, find the beginning of the section Monday, Week I, Morning Prayer in the Psalter of your prayer book. We will assume that it is the First Monday of Advent. Depending on your edition, it is found on the following page:

Shorter Christian Prayer: Page 54

A Shorter Morning and Evening Prayer: Page 44

One-volume *Christian Prayer*: Page 718

Four-volume *Liturgy of the Hours*: Page 702

It will begin with the words:

Morning Prayer

God, come to my assistance. Glory to the Father.
As it was in the beginning. Alleluia.

(If you just prayed the Invitatory, then skip these introductory prayers and go to the hymn, below.) As before, this is not the full text. It serves only as a reminder. The full text is in the Ordinary. Turn there now, keeping a finger (or a ribbon) on Monday, Week I, Morning Prayer. Depending on your book, the introductory prayers for Morning prayer are found in the Ordinary on these pages:

> *Shorter Christian Prayer*: Page 18. NOTE: This abridged edition (correctly) incorporates the Invitatory into Morning Prayer, and does not have text for beginning Morning Prayer with "God, come to my assistance. . . ."

A Shorter Morning and Evening Prayer: Page 20

One-volume *Christian Prayer*: Page 689

Four-volume *Liturgy of the Hours*: Page 653

Stand, make the sign of the cross and pray:

Morning Prayer

God, come to my assistance.
—Lord, make haste to help me.

Glory to the Father, and to the Son, and to the Holy
　Spirit:
as it was in the beginning, is now, and will be forever.
　Amen

Alleluia.

If there are two or more of you praying together, then one would pray the first line, while the other prays the second, and so on.

The "Alleluia" is omitted during Lent.

Hymn (Optional)

Turning back to the Psalter, the listed hymn begins:

> Brightness of the Father's glory . . .

Some one-volume prayer books do not show the hymn text, but include numbers referring to hymns listed in the back of the book. It might also read "Outside Ordinary Time, see Guide" with a page number. This refers to a seasonal list of hymns, so that you can select a hymn appropriate to the current season. (For this example, you would choose a hymn from the Advent section.)

The hymn is optional. It can be sung, chanted, read, substituted or omitted altogether. Sometimes the hymn won't be listed directly, or optional ones will be included. If you include the hymn, it is usually sung standing.

Psalmody

Be seated for the Psalmody, which consists of a Psalm, an Old Testament Canticle, and another Psalm, along with their associated antiphons. For the First Monday of Advent the antiphon is:

> Ant. 1   I lift up my heart to you, O Lord, and you
> will hear my morning prayer.

Go ahead and pray it now. Shorter prayer books may list alternative antiphons for special seasons immediately under the standard one. For example, *Shorter Christian Prayer* lists the following antiphon for Easter directly under the standard antiphon:

> All those who love your name will rejoice in you.
> Alleluia.

PSALMODY

Ant. 1   I lift up my heart to you, O Lord, and you
          will hear my morning prayer.

Psalm 5:2-10, 12-13

A morning prayer asking for help

Those who welcome the Word as the guest of their
hearts will have abiding joy.

To my words give ear, O Lord,
give heed to my groaning.
Attend to the sound of my cries,

. . .

There is text in italics before the Psalm. Do not say this aloud.
Merely reflect upon it for a moment. When the prayer is spoken (and
not sung or chanted) some groups prefer to pray the text in black
italics in place of the antiphon.

Then Psalm 5:2-10,12-13 is said, while seated. If praying with
others, it is common to alternate the praying of individual verses.
Unless noted otherwise, the following is recited after *every* Psalm
and Canticle:

Glory to the Father, and to the Son, and to the Holy
    Spirit:
as it was in the beginning, is now, and will be for ever.
Amen.

Many books will show an optional Psalm-prayer immediately
following the Psalm. However, this does not appear to be the intended order of Liturgy of the Hours. Rather, after the Doxology ("Glory
to the Father . . ."), repeat the antiphon for the Psalm a final time,
observe a moment of reflective silence, then pray the Psalm-prayer.

Psalm-prayer

Lord, all justice and all goodness come from you; you hate evil and abhor lies. Lead us, your servants, in the path of your justice, so that all who hope in you may rejoice with the Church and in Christ.

Ant. 1   I lift up my heart to you, O Lord, and you will hear my morning prayer.

Repeat the above pattern two more times — antiphon, Psalm or Canticle, Doxology, antiphon — followed by Psalm-prayer as indicated. Note that there is not a Psalm-prayer after the Canticle.

Readings

During Ordinary Time the Scripture Reading generally comes next in the text of the Psalter. But because it is Advent (for the sake of the tutorial), it gets a little tricky. For the Scripture Reading we turn to a different section in the prayer book to complete Morning Prayer:

Shorter Christian Prayer: Page 362

A Shorter Morning and Evening Prayer: Page 381

One-volume *Christian Prayer*: Page 47

Four-volume *Liturgy of the Hours*: Page 153

The reading for the First Monday of Advent is Isaiah 2:3 (some will have Isaiah 2:3-4):

Morning Prayer

READING   ISAIAH 2:3

Come, let us climb the Lord's mountain,
to the house of the God of Jacob. . .

Allow a short time of silence following the reading. A brief message or reflection may even be prepared. Normally, a priest or deacon would preach in such a situation, but in their absence, a prepared layperson may give a message.

Responsory (Optional)

The Responsory is sometimes omitted or adapted in private recitation. If you choose to say the Responsory or are praying in a group, then say:

RESPONSORY

Your light will come, Jerusalem; the Lord will dawn on you in radiant beauty.
— Your light will come, Jerusalem; the Lord will dawn on you in radiant beauty.

You will see his glory within you;
— The Lord will dawn on you in radiant beauty.

Glory to the Father, and to the Son, and to the Holy Spirit
— Your light will come, Jerusalem; the Lord will dawn on you in radiant beauty.

In groups, a leader or half of the group recites one line, then the remainder say the line beginning with the dash. Please note that the Responsory, here and elsewhere, is the only prayer in which we pray "Glory to the Father, and to the Son, and to the Holy Spirit" without proceeding to "As it was in the beginning . . ."

Canticle of Zechariah (Gospel Canticle)

The antiphon for the Canticle will be found right after the Responsory. Say it now.

CANTICLE OF ZECHARIAH

Ant Lift up your eyes, Jerusalem, and see the great
    power of your King; your Savior comes to set you
    free.

But where is the Canticle? It's in the Ordinary. Hold this page with
your finger or a ribbon and flip to the Ordinary. Look for the section
on Morning Prayer and find the Canticle of Zechariah (Luke 1:68-
79). Now pray the Canticle following the same form as the Psalms
— together or antiphonally.

   After reciting the Canticle, say:

   Glory to the Father, and to the Son, and to the Holy
      Spirit:
   as it was in the beginning, is now, and will be forever.
      Amen.

And then repeat the antiphon.

Intercessions

Now return to the Proper of the Seasons.

INTERCESSIONS

Christ the Lord, Son of the living God, light from
    light, leads us into the light and reveals his
    holiness. With confidence let us make our prayer:
    Come, Lord Jesus

Light that never fades, dispel the mists about us,
— awaken our faith from sleep.

Guard us from all harm today,
— may your glory fill us with joy.

Give us unfailing gentleness at all times,
— toward everyone we meet. . . .

The intercessions are said while standing after the same pattern as the Responsory. The italics, *"Come, Lord Jesus,"* are sometimes read by the entire group, or they may be treated as a regular response. The intercessions lead directly into the Our Father, which may be preceded by a brief invitation such as:

> And now let us pray as Christ taught us:
> Our Father, who art in heaven . . .

Other options for the invitation are in the Ordinary. The concluding "Amen" is omitted.

Concluding Prayer

The concluding prayer follows immediately without any prefatory words. While standing, say:

Prayer

Lord our God,
help us to prepare
for the coming of Christ your Son.

May he find us waiting,
eager in joyful prayer.

We ask this through our Lord Jesus Christ, your Son,
who lives and reigns with you and the Holy Spirit, one
God, for ever and ever.

Sometimes alternative concluding prayers are provided in the Proper. Pray whichever one you wish.

In individual recitation or when prayed communally without any clergy present, Morning Prayer is ended by making the sign of the cross while praying:

> May the Lord bless us,
> protect us from all evil
> and bring us to everlasting life.
> — Amen.

Make sure the ribbons get placed correctly for your next prayers, and you are finished. The other step-by-step tutorial sections are keyed to the four-volume prayer book set. If you have a shorter edition, make adaptations similar to those mentioned in this tutorial section.

Daytime Prayer Order

Stand

✠ "God, come to my assistance . . ."

Hymn*

Sit

First Antiphon, Psalm and Doxology

First Antiphon*, Silence* and Psalm-Prayer*

Second Antiphon, Psalm and Doxology

Second Antiphon*, Silence* and Psalm-Prayer*

Third Antiphon, Psalm and Doxology

Third Antiphon*, Silence* and Psalm-Prayer*

Scripture Reading

Stand

Concluding Prayer

Daytime Prayer Tutorial

Daytime Prayer (also called Midday Prayer) is prayed between 9:00AM and 3:00PM. The text is found only in the larger prayer volumes.

Daytime Prayer is found, almost in its entirety, in the Psalter. During special seasons, feasts, memorials or the like, the second half of the prayer is in the Proper of the Seasons, the Proper of Saints or the Common.

Introductory Prayers

For this example, find the beginning of the section Monday, Week I, Daytime Prayer in the Psalter of your prayer book. We will assume that it is the First Monday of Advent. It will begin with the words:

Daytime Prayer

God, come to my assistance. Glory to the Father. As it was in the beginning. Alleluia.

Hymn, as in the Ordinary, 658.

As before, this is not the full text. It serves only as a reminder. The full text is found in the Ordinary. Turn there now, keeping a finger (or a ribbon) on Monday, Week I, Daytime Prayer.

While standing, make the sign of the cross and pray:

Daytime Prayer

God, come to my assistance.
—Lord, make haste to help me.

Glory to the Father, and to the Son, and to the Holy Spirit:
as it was in the beginning, is now, and will be forever. Amen. Alleluia.

If there are two or more of you praying together, then one would pray the first line, while the other prays the second, and so on.

The "Alleluia" is omitted during Lent.

Hymn (Optional)

The Psalter refers to a hymn in the Ordinary. There are three sets to choose from; midmorning, midday and midafternoon. Simply choose the hymn most appropriate to your time of day.

The hymn is entirely optional. It can be sung, chanted, read, substituted or omitted altogether. If you include the hymn, it is usually sung standing.

Psalmody

PSALMODY

Antiphon, as in the Proper of Seasons

Psalm 19B

Praise of God who gave us the law of love

You must be perfect as your heavenly Father is perfect (Matthew 5:48).

The law of the Lord is perfect,
it revives the soul.
The rule of the Lord is to be trusted,
it gives wisdom to the simple.

· · ·

Be seated as you turn back to the Psalter for the Psalmody, which consists of three Psalms. Note that the antiphon is missing. The red lettering indicates that the antiphon is in the Proper of Seasons. Turning to the Proper of Seasons, we find that the antiphon, like the hymn, varies depending on the time of day; midmorning, midday or midafternoon. Let us assume it is midday, around noon.

Go ahead and recite the antiphon:

> Ant.   The angel Gabriel said to Mary in greeting:
> Hail, full of grace, the Lord is with you;
> blessed are you among women.

Now return to the Psalter. Notice the text in italics before the Psalm. Do not say this aloud. Merely reflect upon it for a moment. When the prayer is spopken (and not sung or chanted) some groups prefer to pray the text in black italics in place of the antiphon.

Then Psalm 19B is said, while seated. If praying with another, it is common to take turns reading/chanting individual verses.

It might not be listed in your book, but the following is recited after every Psalm and Canticle:

> Glory to the Father, and to the Son, and to the Holy
> Spirit:
> as it was in the beginning, is now, and will be forever.
> Amen.

Some books will show a "Psalm-prayer" immediately following the Psalm. However, this does not appear to be the intended order of Liturgy of the Hours. Rather, after the Doxology ("Glory to the Father . . ."), repeat the antiphon for the first Psalm a final time, observe a brief period of silence, then pray the Psalm-prayer.

Psalm-prayer

May our words in praise of your commandments find favor with you, Lord. May our faith prove we are not slaves, but sons, not so much subjected to your law as sharing your power.

Repeat the above pattern two more times — antiphon, Psalm, Doxology, antiphon — followed by Psalm-prayer as indicated. Antiphon patterns vary for different seasons. In Advent, for example, there appears one antiphon for the entire set of Daytime Prayer Psalm readings. Some people choose to recite this antiphon once at the beginning, and then again only after the conclusion of *all* of the Psalm readings. Others recite the antiphon between each reading. Feel free to proceed as you and your group desire.

Readings and Responsory

Turn again to the Proper of the Seasons to continue. The reading for the First Monday of Advent, Midday, is Isaiah 10:24a, 27:

READING   ISAIAH 10:24A, 27

    Thus says the Lord, the God of hosts:
O my people, who dwell in Zion,
    do not fear.
      On that day,
The burden shall be taken from your shoulder,
    and the yoke shattered from your neck.

Remember us, Lord, because of the love you have
    for your people.
—Come and bring us your salvation.

Notice that the reading is followed by a brief Responsory (indicated by the dash). Observe a short time of silence following the reading, before the Responsory. After the time of silence, recite the Responsory — "Remember us, Lord, because of the love . . ." — then let your eyes follow past the other Daytime readings. Note the text at the end:

    Prayer, as in Morning Prayer.

Concluding Prayer

The concluding prayer from Morning Prayer is one page back in the Proper of Seasons. Turn back to the prayer, stand, and without any prefatory words say:

Prayer

Lord our God,
help us to prepare
for the coming of Christ your Son.
May he find us waiting,
eager in joyful prayer.

We ask this through our Lord Jesus Christ, your Son,
who lives and reigns with you and the Holy Spirit, one
God, for ever and ever. Amen.

As indicated in the Ordinary, when prayed communally, Daytime Prayer concludes with:

Let us praise the Lord.
— And give him thanks.

If you now make sure your ribbons are placed where you left off (in the Proper, Ordinary and Psalter) then you will be able to resume prayer easily later.

Some individuals and groups pray multiple daytime prayers on a single day. However, only one set of Psalms and readings are provided for a given day. Groups that pray multiple daytime prayers generally supplement the Psalms and readings by using materials from other daytime prayers or the Complementary Psalmody.

Evening Prayer Order

Stand

✠ "God, come to my assistance . . ."

Hymn*

Sit

First Antiphon, Psalm and Doxology

First Antiphon*, Silence* and Psalm-Prayer*

Second Antiphon, Psalm and Doxology

Second Antiphon*, Silence* and Psalm-Prayer*

Third Antiphon, New Testament Canticle and Doxology

Third Antiphon*, Silence*

Scripture Reading

Silence* and Message*

Responsory*

Stand

✠ Antiphon, Canticle of Mary and Doxology

Canticle Antiphon*

Intercessions

Our Father

Concluding Prayer and ✠ Blessing

Evening Prayer Tutorial

Evening Prayer is usually prayed between 4:00 and 7:00PM. It is found, almost in its entirety, in the Psalter. (During special seasons, feasts, memorials or the like, the second half of the prayer is in the Proper of the Seasons, the Proper of Saints or the Common.)

Introductory Prayers

in the Psalter of your prayer book find the beginning of the section for Monday, Week I, Evening Prayer. We will assume that it is the First Monday of Advent. It begins with the words:

Evening Prayer

God, come to my assistance. Glory to the Father.
As it was in the beginning. Alleluia.

This is not the full text. It serves only as a reminder. The full text is in the Ordinary. Turn there now, keeping a finger or ribbon on Monday, Week I, Evening Prayer. While standing, make the sign of the cross and pray:

Evening Prayer

God, come to my assistance.
—Lord, make haste to help me.

Glory to the Father, and to the Son, and to the Holy
  Spirit:
as it was in the beginning, is now, and will be forever.
  Amen. Alleluia.

If there are two or more of you praying together, then one would pray the first line, while the other prays the second, and so on.

The "Alleluia" is omitted during Lent.

Hymn (Optional)

The hymn is given in the Psalter. It begins:

> Lord Jesus Christ, abide with us . . .

The hymn is entirely optional. It can be sung, chanted, read, substituted or omitted altogether. Sometimes the hymn won't be listed directly, or optional ones will be included. If you use the hymn, it is usually sung standing.

Psalmody

Be seated for the Psalmody, which consists of two Psalms and a New Testament Canticle along with their associated antiphons. For the First Monday of Advent, the antiphon is:

PSALMODY

Ant. 1   The Lord looks tenderly on those who are poor.

Psalm 11

God is the unfailing support of the just

Blessed are those who hunger and thirst for justice; for they shall be satisfied (Matthew 5:6).

In the Lord I have taken my refuge.
How can you say to my soul:
"Fly like a bird to its mountain. . . ."

Go ahead and pray the antiphon now. Shorter prayer books may list alternative antiphons for special seasons immediately under the standard one. For example, *Shorter Christian Prayer* lists the following antiphon for Easter directly under the standard antiphon:

> Have courage; I have overcome the world. Alleluia.

Notice the text in italics before the Psalm. Do not say this aloud. Merely reflect upon it for a moment. When the prayer is spoken (and not sung or chanted) some groups prefer to pray the text in black italics in place of the antiphon. Then Psalm 11 is said, while seated. If praying with another, it is common to take turns reading or chanting individual verses.

It might not be listed in your book, but the following is recited after *every* Psalm and Canticle:

> Glory to the Father, and to the Son, and to the Holy
>   Spirit:
> as it was in the beginning, is now, and will be forever.
>   Amen.

Some books will show a "Psalm-prayer" immediately following the Psalm. However, this does not appear to be the intended order of Liturgy of the Hours. Rather, after the Doxology ("Glory to the Father . . ."), repeat the antiphon for the first Psalm a final time, then pray the Psalm-prayer.

Psalm-prayer

Lord God, you search the hearts of all, both the good and the wicked. May those who are in danger for love of you find security in you now, and, in the day of judgment, may they rejoice in seeing you face to face.

Ant. 1   The Lord looks tenderly on those who are
         poor.

Repeat the above pattern two more times — antiphon, Psalm, Doxology, antiphon — followed by Psalm-prayer as indicated. Note that there is not a "Psalm-prayer" after the Canticle.

Readings

If you are using a larger volume, it probably now instructs you to turn to the Proper of the Seasons to continue. In some books, a standard reading will follow immediately in the Psalter. However, since this is Advent (for the sake of the tutorial), turn to the Proper of the Seasons, First Week of Advent, Monday, Evening Prayer. (Shorter prayer books may have just a single week of readings for Advent. If this is your situation, use the one for Monday.)

The reading for the First Monday of Advent is from Philippians 3:20b-21:

Evening Prayer

READING   PHILIPPIANS 3:20B-21

We eagerly await the coming of our Savior, the Lord Jesus Christ . . .

Observe a short time of silence following the reading. A short message or reflection may even be prepared. Normally, a priest or deacon would preach in such a situation, but in their absence, laity may give a message.

Responsory (Optional)

The Responsory is sometimes omitted in private recitation. As with other similarly structured prayers, this can be prayed antiphonally.

RESPONSORY

Come and set us free, Lord God of power and might.
— Come and set us free, Lord God of power and might.

Let your face shine upon us and we shall be saved,
— Lord God of power and might.

> Glory to the Father . . .
> — Come and set . . .

Only a part of the final response is shown. The full text is identical to the first line of the Responsory. Note again that, in the Responsory (see page 54), you pray only the first part of the usual "Glory to the Father."

Canticle of Mary (Gospel Canticle)

The antiphon for the Canticle is found right after the Responsory:

> CANTICLE OF MARY
>
> Ant   The angel of the Lord brought God's message to Mary, and she conceived by the power of the Holy Spirit, alleluia.

But where is the Canticle? It's in the Ordinary.

Mark this page with your finger (or a ribbon) and flip to the Ordinary. Look for Evening Prayer and you should soon find the Canticle of Mary (Luke 1:46-55). Stand, make the sign of the cross, recite the antiphon, then recite the Canticle together or taking turns at reading individual verses as you wish.

After reciting the Canticle, say:

> Glory to the Father, and to the Son, and to the Holy Spirit:
> as it was in the beginning, is now, and will be forever.
> Amen.

Then repeat the antiphon and return to the Proper of the Seasons to continue with the Intercessions.

Intercessions

> INTERCESSIONS
>
> We cry to the Lord, who will come to bring us
> salvation.
> *Come, Lord, and save us.*
> Lord Jesus Christ, our God, Savior of all,
> — come swiftly and save us.
> Lord, by your coming into this world,
> — free us from the sin of the world.
> You came from the Father,
> — show us the path that leads to him.
> You were conceived by the Holy Spirit,
> — by your word renew the same spirit in our hearts.
> You became incarnate from the Virgin Mary,
> — free our bodies from corruption.
> Lord, be mindful of all men,
> — who from the beginning of time have placed their
> trust in you.

The intercessions are said while standing. The italics, *"Come, Lord, and save us,"* are sometimes read by the entire group, or they may be treated as a regular response. The intercessions lead directly into the Our Father, which may be preceded by a brief invitation, for example:

> And now let us pray as Christ taught us:
> Our Father, who art in heaven . . .

Other options are given in the Ordinary. The concluding "Amen" is omitted.

Concluding Prayer

The concluding prayer follows immediately without any prefatory words. While standing, say:

Prayer

Lord our God,
help us to prepare
for the coming of Christ your Son.
May he find us waiting,
eager in joyful prayer.

We ask this through our Lord Jesus Christ, your Son,
who lives and reigns with you and the Holy Spirit, one
God, for ever and ever.

In individual recitation or when prayed communally without any priest present, Evening Prayer ends, as shown in the Ordinary, by making the sign of the cross while praying:

May the Lord bless us,
protect us from all evil
and bring us to everlasting life.
— Amen.

This concludes Evening Prayer.

Night Prayer Order

Stand

✠ "God, come to my assistance. . . ."

Examination of Conscience

Hymn*

Sit

First Antiphon, Psalm and Doxology

First Antiphon*

Second Antiphon, Psalm and Doxology

Second Antiphon*

Scripture Reading

Silence*

Responsory*

Stand

✠ Antiphon, Canticle of Simeon and Doxology

Canticle Antiphon*

Prayer

Conclusion

Antiphon in Honor of the Blessed Virgin

Night Prayer Tutorial

Night Prayer is prayed shortly before bedtime. It has only a one-week cycle, and is in its own section, usually at or near the end of the Psalter. Go ahead and turn to Night Prayer now.

Introductory Prayers

Assuming that it is the First Monday of Advent, find the Night Prayer for Monday. The first thing we are instructed to do is to turn to the Ordinary, where we see that Night Prayer begins with:

Night Prayer

God, come to my assistance.
—Lord, make haste to help me.

Glory to the Father, and to the Son, and to the Holy
   Spirit:
as it was in the beginning, is now, and will be forever.
   Amen. Alleluia.

If there are two or more of you praying together, then one would pray the first line, while the other prays the second, and so on. These introductory prayers are prayed while standing.

The "Alleluia" is omitted during Lent.

Examination of Conscience

Take a moment to think back through the day and recall those times when you failed to love others as Christ has loved us. Offer these to God, seeking his forgiveness.

In communal prayer, some groups will also use the penitential prayer from the Mass. ("Lord have mercy. Christ have mercy. Lord have mercy.")

Hymn (Optional)

The Ordinary instructs us to turn to a different part of the Psalter to find the hymn. This is actually a collection of hymns. Feel free to select one you like.

The hymn is entirely optional. It can be sung, chanted, read, substituted or omitted altogether. If you include the hymn, it is usually sung standing.

Psalmody

Be seated for the Psalmody, which consists of one or two Psalms with their associated antiphons. In this case the antiphon is:

Ant.   O Lord, our God, unwearied is your love for us.

Go ahead and pray the antiphon.

PSALMODY

Ant.   O Lord, our God, unwearied is your love for us.

Psalm 86

Poor man's prayer in trouble

Blessed be God who comforts us in all our trials (2 Corinthians 1:3, 4).

Turn your ear, O Lord, and give answer
for I am poor and needy.
Preserve my life, for I am faithful:
save the servant who trusts in you. . . .

Notice the italic text before the Psalm. Do not say this aloud. Merely reflect upon it for a moment. When the prayer is spoken (and not sung or chanted) some groups prefer to pray the text in black italics in place of the antiphon.

Then Psalm 86 is said while seated. If praying with another, it is common to take turns reading/chanting individual verses.

Unless noted otherwise, the Doxology is recited after *every* Psalm and Canticle:

> Glory to the Father, and to the Son, and to the Holy
>   Spirit:
> as it was in the beginning, is now, and will be forever.
>   Amen.

Repeat the antiphon after the Doxology. When the Night Prayer includes a second Psalm, recite Antiphon 2, then the Psalm, the Doxology, and Antiphon 2 again.

Readings

The reading for this Monday is 1 Thessalonians 5:9-10.

READING   1 THESSALONIANS 5:9-10

God has destined us for acquiring salvation through our Lord Jesus Christ. He died for us, that all of us, whether awake or asleep, together might live with him.

It is not uncommon to have a short time of silence following the reading.

Responsory (optional)

In individual recitation, people often say only the first line of each couplet from the Responsory. Feel free to pray it as is appropriate to your group.

RESPONSORY

Into your hands, Lord, I commend my spirit.
—Into your hands, Lord, I commend my spirit.

You have redeemed us, Lord God of truth.
—I commend my spirit.

Glory to the Father . . .
—Into your hands, Lord, I commend my spirit.

Canticle of Simeon (Gospel Canticle)

The antiphon for the Canticle will be found right after the Responsory. Stand, make the sign of the cross and say:

Ant. Protect us, Lord, as we stay awake; watch
over us as we sleep, that awake, we may keep
watch with Christ, and asleep, rest in his peace.

Then pray the Canticle. The title in red type is not read:

GOSPEL CANTICLE   LUKE 2:29-32

Christ is the light of the nations and the glory of Israel

Lord, now you let your servant go in peace;
your word has been fulfilled:

my own eyes have seen the salvation
which you have prepared in the sight of every people:

a light to reveal you to the nations
and the glory of your people Israel.

After reciting the Canticle, say:

Glory to the Father, and to the Son, and to the Holy
Spirit:
as it was in the beginning, is now, and will be forever.
Amen.

And then repeat the antiphon.

Concluding Prayers

The concluding prayer, given in the Psalter, follows immediately, without any prefatory words. While standing, say:

> Lord,
> give our bodies restful sleep
> and let the work we have done today
> bear fruit in eternal life.
> We ask this through Christ our Lord.

. . . and then . . .

> May the all-powerful Lord grant us a restful night and
> a peaceful death.
> —Amen.

Antiphon in Honor of the Blessed Virgin

The last part of Night Prayer is a brief antiphon in honor of Mary. Whether you are following from the Ordinary or from the Night Prayer section of the Psalter, it will usually direct you to another page that has a list of short prayers.

Choose from any of those provided in your prayer book. They are read, chanted, or sometimes sung.

Seasons, Memorials, Feasts and Solemnities

The easiest way to learn the Liturgy of the Hours is to simply pray the prayers straight through as found in the Psalter. This is how the prayers are usually recited during the "Ordinary Time" of the year. This requires little or no page flipping and is not difficult to follow. We recommend that you pray in this way until you become familiar with the sequence of the daily offices and the use of your prayer book. Once you have mastered praying from the Psalter, and have good command of the sequence of the standard prayer elements, then it is time to integrate the complete calendar of the Liturgy.

In the Church's calendar there are four seasons in addition to Ordinary Time: Advent, Christmas, Lent and Easter. There are also specific celebrations of historical events and individuals recognized on particular days. The purpose of these seasons and days is to remind us throughout the entire year of Christ's life, death and resurrection, and to call to mind particular people and events that exemplify his transforming grace.

> Feast Days, or Holy Days, are days which are celebrated in commemoration of the sacred mysteries and events recorded in the history of our redemption, in memory of the Virgin Mother of Christ, or of His apostles, martyrs, and saints, by special services and rest from work. A feast not only commemorates an event or person, but also serves to excite the spiritual life by reminding us of the event it commemorates. At certain hours Jesus Christ invites us to His vineyard (Matt., xx, 1-15); He is born in our hearts at Christmas; on Good Friday we nail ourselves to the cross with Him; at Easter we rise from the tomb of sin; and at Pentecost we receive the gifts of the Holy Ghost. Every religion has its feasts, but none has such a rich and judiciously constructed system of festive seasons as the Catholic Church. The succession of these seasons form the

ecclesiastical year, in which the feasts of Our Lord form the ground and framework, the feasts of the Blessed Virgin and the Saints the ornamental tracery. (*New Catholic Encyclopedia*)

These particular celebrations are collectively called "feasts" or "feast days." They are categorized in terms of their centrality to the faith, from least to greatest, as memorials, feasts or solemnities (there are additional divisions and categories, but for the sake of simplicity we will leave it at three). Although even the smallest prayer books have a few alternative prayers and antiphons for special seasons and days, only the larger prayer books have comprehensive prayers for specific memorials, feasts and solemnities. The prayers and readings during these special seasons and days are adjusted to relate to the celebration and help us to meditate upon it.

There are three questions in regard to following the calendar: knowing which seasonal or feast day it is, finding the prayers for the day in question, and deciding what to do when multiple feasts fall on the same day.

An Example

Imagine it is Monday, December 13, 2004, and we would like to pray Morning Prayer. If we are not aware that December 13 is a memorial day (or we don't have a prayer book that includes memorials), we might just pray the prayers for Monday of the third week of Advent. By checking a Church calendar or the Proper of the Saints, we see that December 13 is the memorial of Lucy, virgin and martyr. So how does this Memorial affect our prayers for this day?

Prior to beginning our prayers, page through the prayers in the Proper of the Saints for December 13. There is a short introduction to Lucy, and then some text that reads (from the four-volume set):

From the common of martyrs, 1401, or virgins, 1473.

Following the above text is a replacement second reading and Responsory for the Office of Readings, a Canticle antiphon and closing prayer for Morning Prayer, and a Canticle antiphon for Evening Prayer.

In general, any prayer element specific to a feast day replaces the same element in the Psalter, Ordinary or Proper of Seasons. Antiphons replace antiphons, readings replace readings, intercessions replace intercessions, etc. This means that for Morning Prayer, we are to use the Canticle antiphon and closing prayer from the section on Lucy, and turn to the Common of Martyrs or Virgins for other replacement prayer elements.

We can use either the Common of Martyrs or the Common of Virgins, but not both. For this example let's use the Common of Martyrs. Turn to 1401, and skip forward several pages to Morning Prayer, where we find an entry that includes a hymn, antiphons and other elements of Morning Prayer. These are substitutions for the same parts in the standard Morning Prayer for the day. So we pray from the Psalter for Monday of Advent, Week 3 as we normally would, but we substitute different antiphons and other elements from the Common of Martyrs. When we come to the Canticle of Zechariah or the concluding prayer, we use those specified not by the Common of Martyrs, but the ones specific to Lucy on page 1245. If you explore the prayers for a feast or solemnity, you will find a similar pattern, but usually with more substitutionary text.

Solemnities are Special

Solemnities require more forethought than feasts and memorials. Solemnities actually begin on the evening prior to the date for the solemnity, itself — at the Vigil. Let's review the Solemnity of the Immaculate Conception, which falls on December 8. Turning to December 8 in the Proper of the Saints, the first prayer listed is Evening Prayer I. Just as on Sunday, Evening Prayer I is the Evening Prayer for the night before the day in question, so observance of the Solemnity of the Immaculate Conception actually begins on the evening of December 7. If you didn't figure this out until December 8, you were late to the party!

Like our previous example with the memorial of Lucy, the Proper of the Saints provides elements that substitute for the antiphons and other portions of the usual prayers, beginning with Evening Prayer for December 7, and proceeding through the Evening Prayer for June 8.

But wait . . . there's more . . .

Solemnities (and a few other celebrations) can sneak up on you not only by beginning their observance earlier than you might have suspected, but also by not always falling on the same calendar date. For example, consider the Solemnity of Corpus Christi, which is on June 10 in 2004. If you look for this in the Proper of the Saints, you won't find it. There is no entry for June 10. The reason for this is that some celebrations are set not for the same date each year, but for a day *in relation to another key date,* such as Easter or Christmas. These date-relative celebrations, the "moveable feasts," are usually found in a section near the end of the Proper of the Seasons, not in the Proper of the Saints.

This can make it a little confusing at times, but an easy solution is to consult a liturgical calendar prior to beginning your prayers for any given day, looking not only at the prayers for today, but checking to see if the following day is a solemnity.

Solemnities are not merely days to observe when praying the Liturgy of the Hours. They are also usually Holy Days of Obligation, so be sure to get to Mass! (In some cases a diocese or national conference suppresses them or moves their observance to the nearest Sunday. Check with your local parish or diocese for information specific to your area.)

Solemnities and Smaller Prayer Books

Smaller prayer books contain sections with alternative antiphons, readings, and so forth, not only for special seasons and particular solemnities, but also for Sundays in Ordinary Time. So during special seasons, solemnities, Sundays, and even some feasts, look to the supplemental sections of your prayer books for alternative prayer elements.

Do I have to do *all* of this?

Thankfully, no. Remember: Laity are encouraged to pray *part* of the Liturgy of the Hours or an adaptation thereof. Your priest is strongly encouraged to make at least Evening Prayer publicly available once a week at the parish, which gives you a useful indicator of the Church's expectations regarding lay participation. At times you will probably draw satisfaction from praying the Liturgy fully or "accurately," but most laity do not find themselves in a state of life that allows for one or two hours of prayer each day.

Different religious orders, dioceses and national conferences have different regulations regarding the observance of particular feasts, and which prayers are required to be prayed and when. Some are quite rigorous. In general, permanent deacons and some in religious orders are obligated to pray Morning and Evening prayer daily. Priests, bishops, and many religious orders vow to pray all of the daily prayers in their entirety. Some orders even pray additional prayers that were removed from the daily schedule for historical reasons. Those who are *obligated* to pray the Hours are to do so properly, following the calendar of seasons and feasts.

When Feasts Collide

If you wish to accurately follow the calendar of feasts (and have a book with the appropriate sections to do so), the rules are detailed in the Church's "General Instruction of the Liturgy of the Hours." In summary, if there is no feast for a particular day, then you just pray the regular prayers for the day. If there is an optional memorial on the day, then *you* choose between the regular prayers and the optional memorial. If there is a regular memorial, feast or solemnity, then you pray the associated prayers. Most calendars use capitalization to indicate the kind of feast day:

- SOLEMNITY (all capitals)
- FEAST (small capitals)
- Memorial (regular text)
- *Optional Memorial* (italics)

Sometimes multiple feasts will fall on the same day. See the Table of Liturgical Days in the "General Instruction" for the specifics on which celebrations take precedence when multiple ones fall on the same day. Though there are some exceptions, in general the order of precedence is:

1. Major seasonal liturgical days and solemnities, such as Easter Triduum and Octave of Easter, Christmas, Epiphany, Ascension, Pentecost, Ash Wednesday, Holy Week, etc.
2. Other solemnities, which includes Sundays
3. Feasts
4. Obligatory memorials
5. "Standard" readings or optional memorials

If multiple celebrations fall on the same day, you simply pick the highest from the list. Suppose, for example, that it is January 4, 2004. Several possible prayers intersect on this day; Epiphany (a solemnity and liturgical day), Sunday of Christmas season, the obligatory memorial of Elizabeth Ann Seton (in the Americas), and the regular Sunday prayer of the Psalter. If you have the four-volume set, prayers are available therein to observe all of these celebrations. Which one would you celebrate?

According to the above table, Epiphany takes precedence over the other celebrations, so you would look to the Proper of the Seasons for Epiphany, and follow the prayers found there.

Church calendars often include information on feast days that fall on Sunday or on days with greater feasts for informative purposes only. Other calendars purposefully and rightly omit feasts and memorials from the calendar when they fall on a Sunday or on the same day on which a greater feast is observed. This is because we are to observe only one feast on a given day, the most solemn one of the day in question. Obviously, the Lord's Day always takes precedence over feasts and memorials (and most other solemnities). Therefore, on Sundays we will almost always be praying the prayers for that Sunday, not the prayers for a feast or memorial that happened to fall on Sunday. And on days with multiple feasts we pray the most important feast for that day.

In outline form, we follow this pattern when preparing to pray:

1. Determine the current season and any special feast that should be observed today (including "Sunday" observances). For this you can use the calendars provided by many parishes. *The St. Joseph Guide* also has this information, as does a calendar available online from the Apostolate of Prayer. (See resource list at back of book.)

2. See if your prayer book has special materials for today's celebration. All of the prayer books have supplementary sections for the seasons of Advent, Christmas, Lent and Easter, as well as Sundays of Ordinary Time, and major solemnities. Some include a few feasts. The four-volume edition includes optional and obligatory memorials. The changes may be as small as a different antiphon for the Gospel Can-

ticle or a different concluding prayer, or as complete as a nearly total replacement of the standard readings.

3. Begin the prayer, incorporating the special amendments due to the season or feast. If there is no special season or feast, or your prayer book does not include the relevant information, then just pray the standard prayers for the day.

Hymns, Singing and Chant

Hymns

Each office includes a hymn near the beginning. Some have several from which to choose. In the four-volume set, the hymn text is included with the prayer text. In other versions, hymn numbers are given that refer to a hymn section near the back of the book. *Christian Prayer* (the large, one-volume edition) includes melody lines with hymn verses, useful to those who can sight read music. Other editions have only the text for hymns, useful to those who already know the melodies.

If you wish to sing the hymns — especially if you would like to play organ or piano with them — we recommend a supplementary book. *Hymnal for the Hours* (GIA Publications) includes complete music for the hymns found in the Liturgy of the Hours. It also includes tones for common Psalms and antiphons.

Singing and Chant

The Liturgy of the Hours — and the Psalms in particular — were written to be sung. The exact method of singing prayers varies with time, place, ability, culture and context. A method of singing prayer common in the Catholic Church is chant (also known as plainchant or plainsong). Like almost any genre of music, chant can be as difficult or easy as one chooses, but we're going to keep the instructions here very simple. You don't need to be able to read music, play an instrument, or even sing well to participate in and benefit from chant as we introduce it here.

By singing in prayer, a person can experience worship in ways not readily accessible by spoken prayer. But many people feel a little uncomfortable, self-conscious or perhaps embarrassed about singing. Although we hope you will try chanting the prayers, if after a week or so you find it continues to distract you from the words, go back to reading them. It may be that chant just isn't right for you, or perhaps the time and place make it inconvenient.

It is also possible that a more comprehensive introduction to chant would make it more interesting. If you seek additional chanting examples and formation, we recommend *Liber Usualis*, reprinted by St. Bonaventure Publications. *The Adoremus Hymnal*, published by Ignatius Press, also has some helpful examples of chant, but both it and *Liber Usualis* assume a significant mastery of music, including the ability to read plainchant and modern music notation.

Why Chant at All?

As is often the case, the Church and her saints have already answered this question better than the author can, so let us refer to an excerpt from the Preface to the Vatican Edition of *Roman Chant*:

> Holy Mother the Church has received from God the charge of training the souls of the faithful in all holiness, and for this noble end has ever made a happy use of the help of the sacred Liturgy. Wherein — in order that men's minds may not be sundered by differences, but that, on the contrary, the unity which gives vigour and beauty to the mystical body of Christ might flourish unimpaired — she has been zealous to keep the traditions of our forefathers, ever trying diligently to discover and boldly to restore any which might have been forgotten in the course of the ages.

> Now among those things which most nearly touch the sacred Liturgy, being as it were interwoven therein and giving it splendour and impressiveness, the first place must be assigned to the Sacred Chant. We have, indeed, all learnt from experience that it gives a certain breadth to divine worship and uplifts the mind in wondrous wise to heavenly things. Wherefore the Church has never ceased to recommend the use of the Chant, and has striven with the greatest assiduity and diligence to prevent its decline from its pristine dignity.

To this end liturgical music must possess those characteristics which make it preeminently sacred and adapted to the good of souls. It must surely emphasize above all else the dignity of divine worship, and at the same time be able to express pleasantly and truly the sentiments of the Christian soul. It must also be catholic, answering to the needs of every people, country and age, and combine simplicity with artistic perfection. . . .

If anyone is now feeling a little shortchanged by the quality of the music at his or her parish, here is your chance in your private prayer life to benefit from the Church's rich musical heritage. Who knows, maybe your parish's music group would like to learn, too.

A Starting Point for Chant

In modern music we are accustomed to a beat, tempo or rhythm. We break and stretch words and syllables so that they fit a metered form, and usually some kind of rhyming pattern. Consider the children's song, "Mary had a Little Lamb." Each syllable is broken so that it falls on a beat:

> Ma - ry had a lit - tle lamb . . .

In chant, the rhythm is the words, themselves. It isn't a regular, clock-like beat as much as an organic movement, like waves on a shore. Simple chant is almost identical to speaking except that one speaks the words at a constant pitch. For our main example, turn to the first Psalm for Week I, Monday, Morning Prayer (Psalm 5):

> To my words give ear, O Lord,
> give heed to my groaning. . . .

Without difficulty, almost anyone can chant these words at one continuous pitch. Try doing so at a speed slightly slower than normal speech. The exact pitch is not important as long as you can keep the pitch fairly level. If you are praying with others, the pitch needs to be in a range that others can match — not too high or too low. Ex-

tremes can make the prayer feel and sound strained and unpleas-
ant. Pick your normal talking voice, and go up *a little*.

It is common to chant more slowly than the same words would
be spoken, especially the final word in a sentence. Don't chant more
quickly than you would speak the same words to a group. If praying
with others, you may have to slow down even more so that everyone
can stay together.

Breathe as necessary. For our purposes, the exact point at which
you inhale is not very important and will come naturally, usually at
the end of a line or after a punctuation mark.

The next step is to change pitch on the second line. For this
example, raise the pitch slightly as you chant, "give heed . . ." Go
ahead and try it.

> To my words give ear, O Lord,
> give heed to my groaning.

In conversational English, continuous thoughts generally conclude with a slight drop in pitch. It is similar in chant. In the following
four-line stanza, repeat the pitch pattern we used above for lines one
and two when chanting lines three and four, but conclude by drop-
ping down in pitch on the final word, "God."

> To my words give ear, O Lord,
> give heed to my groaning.
> Attend to the sound of my cries,
> my King and my God.

Now try going through the entire Psalm 5, applying these simple
principles. For the three-line stanza, "Lead me Lord . . ." use the
same pitch on the last two lines, but drop in pitch slightly for the final
syllables. With only a little practice, most people find the effect of
even such simple chant "gives a certain breadth to" prayer.

Antiphons

The antiphon is, among other things, an opportunity to announce the tones for the Psalm that follows. If chanting with others, a common way to proceed is for one person to chant the antiphon, which the group repeats. The leader then chants the first stanza of the Psalm. The group copies the leader's tones for the second stanza. They alternate stanzas. This is not the only way to proceed, but a suggestion for when the group is first learning to chant.

Common Variations

OPENING AND CLOSING TONE VARIATIONS

Rather than praying an entire line on one pitch, then the second line on a different pitch, it can be nice to adjust to the new pitch on the last word of the first line. It is also common to have the first word or two start one or two steps below the pitch for the rest of the line.

EXTENDING THE TONES

Instead of alternating the tone on each line, you can extend a tone further. For example, you could extend the tone from the first line through the second line, or even across an entire stanza.

PSALM TONE PATTERN CHANGES

As you have certainly guessed by now, the very simplified tone patterns we've proposed are only a few of thousands of possibilities. There is no reason that you could not try different tonal patterns. Sticking with the same tone day in and day out can become tiresome. Some variation can improve attentiveness while praying.

Canticles

The Canticles of Zechariah and Mary are also likely to be sung or chanted. Most Psalm tones are suitable to either, but it is common to have tones specific to the Canticles.

Praying Perfectly

Please remember this: It is important that you pray perfectly, not sing, chant, or perform perfectly. This is a vital distinction. Contrary to popular belief, your "perfection" is not to do all things without error, but to become fully who you are meant to be, or to engage in something as fully as you are able. To pray perfectly, then, does not mean that you do so with precision, dead-on pitch and exact articulation, but in such a way that it truly involves your entire self, offering your heart, mind and body to God. Singing and chanting prayer is but one way to move toward this goal.

Starting a Prayer Group

Starting or joining a Liturgy of the Hours prayer group in your area may not be difficult. Here is a step-by-step guide on how to do so.

1. To Start or Join?

First things first: Do a little research to see if there is already a Liturgy of the Hours prayer group in your area that meets at a time and place convenient to you.

- Call your local parish.
- Talk with other Catholics at work or in your neighborhood.
- Contact your Diocesan office, and check the event calendars of periodicals they publish.
- If there is a convent or monastery nearby, they might be able to meet your needs.

However, you might not find any groups in your area. Maybe those that exist do not meet at a time or place convenient to you, or perhaps there is something about the group that does not suit your personality. In such cases, it may be time to start one.

2. Find Interested Others

The next step, assuming that you are already familiar with the Liturgy of the Hours, is to find a handful of other people who are interested in praying together. This may not be easy at first, but consider your immediate social group. Are there people in your peer group — family, neighbors, coworkers, friends — who might be interested and who have a schedule similar to your own? Probably.

If so, ask a few of them if they would be interested in spending twenty minutes a week growing closer to God through prayer. Some may be too busy or not understand what you are asking. Some may say yes, but then not show.

Let us correct a common confusion at this point: The difference between prayer and Bible study groups. The two are quite different! A decent Bible study group requires special texts, home-reading, and lots of preparation on the part of one or more leaders. Some people will assume that you are asking them to join a Bible study, and may hesitate based on their assumptions about what it may require, or because of poor past experiences with Bible study groups. Another source of hesitation will come from wondering what, exactly, the purpose of the prayer group will be, or from unfamiliarity with prayer groups in general. If there is already a Bible study taking place, people may wonder what the point is of a prayer group. Some might even suspect that you are making a subtle statement about the inadequacy of the Bible study. Finally, there is the unfortunate human inclination to simply avoid prayer.

3. Get Your Materials

Order a tutorial such as this one and a prayer book for each person who is interested in participating. You may want to purchase a couple of extra prayer books, as people may begin to drop in on the prayer meetings unexpectedly. Ideally, your core group will pool their money for this initial purchase. By making the purchase first, participants will be more likely to follow through on their commitment.

4. Arrange a Location and Weekly Time

It is important that the chosen location be free of distractions, not be disruptive to others, and not cause a conflict with those who are responsible for managing and maintaining the space. Some possibilities include:

- Someone's home
- Local parks or trails (weather willing)
- Library or private office meeting rooms
- Unused classrooms
- Local churches and chapels (perhaps even non-Catholic ones)

You should be able to find a location that does not cost anything. If the room or building you are using is not your own, it is important that the meeting first be cleared with the building management, and that the prayer meeting not interfere with other people's routines.

The meeting location and life-style of your core group members will dictate the timing of the meetings. Common times include:

- Before work (Morning Prayer or Office of Readings)
- Morning, lunch or afternoon break (Daytime Prayer)
- After work (Evening Prayer)
- Mid- or Late-evening (Night Prayer)
- Any other time of day that is convenient

If you can meet together more frequently than once a week, that is fine, but be sure not to attempt too much at the beginning. Doing so may cause people to drop from the group who would otherwise benefit greatly from praying together.

Write down the meeting times on your calendar!

5. Appoint a Prayer Leader

It is important that your prayer group have the right leader for the first few gatherings. This person will likely be the one who is initiating the group, perhaps you. In any case, the prayer leader should be especially familiar with the Liturgy of the Hours, but also be a good and personable teacher. He or she will help people follow the prayers in the right order.

Once your group is generally familiar with the prayers, rather than having a single person lead the group, it is common for the group to divide into two halves. Then the "halves" alternate verses, prayers, readings, etc., throughout the prayer. Still, a single person should remain responsible for coordinating the group and initiating many of the prayers. It is recommended that this responsibility be rotated among the regular attendees, but don't push leadership responsibility on anyone who does not want it.

6. Begin Praying Together

Remind each person in your core group of the prayer meeting a day or two ahead of time, especially for the first couple of months. Individually or as a group, go through the tutorial(s) that apply to your prayer meeting. Make a personal commitment to stick with it for at least one month.

Turn off pagers and cell phones during prayer time. Otherwise, they will surely ring, beep, play annoying tunes or vibrate at the most inopportune moments.

Always be respectful of other people's time. Start and end promptly, but be courteous and welcoming to those who might arrive late. Make a place for them to sit, have someone show them where you are in the prayers, and so forth.

Questions will arise in the process of learning the prayers. Work through these as best you can, remembering that the efficacy of the prayer is not determined by how elegantly you pray, or what gestures or postures are assumed, but by being open to what God wants to do in your life. This book can help by serving as a neutral reference to settle disputes about specific procedures.

7. Invite Others to Join

Once your core group is comfortable with the prayers, it is time to open the group up to others. There is an unfortunate tendency in small groups for them to become introverted and inhospitable to new participants. One way to avoid this is to take a *brief* moment before prayer to welcome newcomers, and then minimize social discussion during your prayer meetings. Participants should commit themselves to making others feel welcome and to helping others learn and participate in the prayers.

8. Group Growth

Healthy prayer groups will grow and multiply. Unhealthy ones will stagnate, fracture and eventually fall apart. As your group grows, you may find that you are outgrowing your facilities, or that another time and place have become convenient for part of the group.

Do not be afraid of spawning new group times at new locations. Participants should feel free to shift from group to group, as all such prayer is participation in the universal prayer of the Church. The need for additional meeting times and locations is a very good sign.

You may also find that, due to any number of factors, a particular meeting time is no longer convenient to the group, and participation will drop. If the reason for lack of participation is the time or location, then change so as to accommodate people's schedules. However, if there is another reason for the low participation, try to honestly discern what that is and address it.

Special Considerations

EMPLOYEE PROGRAMS

Some companies have special programs for non-work-related employee groups. If your company has such programs, this may be an opportunity to introduce your prayer group to others.

EMPLOYER RELATIONS

If your prayer group is meeting on company property, or if employees are leaving the company site to pray, it is imperative that the prayer time not present any conflict with normal company business. Company materials and time should not be used to promote your prayer group. Any postings, communications or e-mails should be approved in advance.

In some companies, prayer groups may generate opposition. To avoid this, insofar as is possible, make sure the group focuses on praying together, and not engaging in other work-related activities as a group. Don't draw unnecessary attention to the group, or show preference in the workplace to other prayer participants.

ECUMENISM

In modern use, "Ecumenism" refers to the dialogue between Christian communities who hold differing doctrinal beliefs, or who have been separated to varying degrees by historical events. The ultimate purpose of Ecumenism is unity. It is perfectly acceptable for Christians not in full communion with Catholicism to pray the Liturgy of the Hours. This is a singular opportunity to share with separated brothers and sisters the Christocentric nature of Catholicism and Catholic prayer.

It is unlikely that most Christians would object to the group or the prayers. However, it should be clear that the Liturgy of the Hours is the prayer of the Catholic Church. In it are found writings not only from Scripture, but from the saints and the Church as well. For example, certain Christians might raise objections to the Marian prayers found in Night Prayer. Be prepared for this if you are praying Night Prayer in an ecumenical setting. There is a sample handout on page 101 for this purpose.

INTERFAITH PARTICIPATION

"Interfaith" refers to relationships between distinct religions; Christianity, Islam, Judaism, Hinduism, and so forth. The Liturgy of the Hours assumes that the participant is Catholic, and although separated Christians will still be able to relate to and participate in it, the Liturgy of the Hours will rarely be appropriate for interfaith meetings. The disparity of belief is simply too great.

CHARISMS OF THE SPIRIT

Many Catholics and other Christians are particularly blessed by charisms of the Spirit such as "tongues," in which they pray in an unknown language. In general, this activity is not appropriate to a liturgical service. However, if the group is open to it, there is not necessarily anything wrong with a short time of such prayer as part of your prayer group meeting before, during or after the Liturgy of the Hours.

THE INEVITABLE OPPOSITION

Prayer is a very good thing, so anticipate opposition. When it is time to gather to pray, your mind will suddenly discover a thousand other things it needs or wants to do. Distractions and temptations will pop up like weeds. This can happen before prayer, or even during prayer. Remember that a consistent habit of prayer is vital to your life with Christ, and that it is only 20 minutes out of your week (or day). Almost any distraction can wait 20 minutes.

Sometimes opposition to prayer will come from within the group. People who are willing to take time out of their day to pray together are frequently sincere and intense, sometimes to the point of making others feel a little uncomfortable. It may be that disagreements arise about how particular parts of the Liturgy of the Hours should be prayed, or what postures and gestures are appropriate. In such cases, the group should be reminded that, for laity, the entire prayer is optional. Laity are free to adapt it to their needs. However, it is good to follow the "General Instruction," and in those areas where the instruction is ambiguous, the group is encouraged to internally agree on a norm. In any event, there are few concrete rules about how laity should (or should not) pray the Liturgy of the Hours. Make every effort to remain charitable and avoid conflict.

Finally, people are instinctively attracted to those things that will improve them. We all hunger for conversion. But people bring with them a variety of baggage. It may happen that a very disordered person joins the group. Do whatever you can to help the person. Be welcoming, charitable, compassionate. Perhaps it is through your group or some people in the group that God intends to bring about that person's conversion. Perhaps he is there to bring needed insight and conversion to others, maybe even yourself.

If it comes to a point that the group is self-destructing as a consequence of one person's presence, someone should gently confront him. If it doesn't help, then a small handful of group leaders might do so together. Finally, failing all else, the group may be forced, sadly, to ask him to leave.

You are invited to pray with us

When? _____ to _____

Where? _____

_____

We will be praying the "Liturgy of the Hours," a traditional Christian Prayer based on passages from the Bible and spiritual meditations of great Christians throughout history.

All materials will be provided.

Please contact _____ at

_____ if you wish to attend.

There is no commitment necessary to participate.

Praying with the Saints

Throughout Christian history people have believed that those who die at peace with God go to heaven to be with him. Though all Christians may be called saints, the word especially applies to those who are already in heaven with Jesus.

A person's love for us doesn't end when they go to heaven, but becomes even more intense, and so we know that these people who loved us while on earth continue to love and care for us from heaven, where they continually commune with, praise and pray to God.

In Catholicism and other Christian expressions it is believed that we can speak to these friends in heaven. Just as we might ask someone on earth to pray for us to God, we can make the same request of the saints. And so the practice of "praying with" or "praying to" the saints has existed in Christianity for many, many centuries.

Some Christians, unfamiliar with the history or reasons for this practice, find it troubling. Because they believe that all prayer is worship, any prayer not "directed to" God seems to them inappropriate at best. But communication with the saints — asking them to pray to God on our behalf — is obviously not a form of worship. So Catholics and other Christians who pray to saints rightly see no conflict or problem with the practice.

If you have additional questions about prayer or the Catholic faith, we encourage you to talk with your prayer group organizer, or a local Catholic priest.

Recommended Resources

Editions of the Liturgy of the Hours

Christian Prayer, Catholic Book Publishing Company, 1999. ISBN 0899424066. *Large Print Edition*, ISBN 0899424074

The Liturgy of the Hours: Complete Set, Leather Cover, Catholic Book Publishing Company, 1999. ISBN 0899424112

The Liturgy of the Hours: Complete Set, Vinyl Cover, Catholic Book Publishing Company, 1980. ISBN 0899424090

The Liturgy of the Hours: Advent and Christmas, Catholic Book Publishing Company, 1980. ISBN 0899424015

The Liturgy of the Hours: Lent and Easter, Catholic Book Publishing Company, 1980. ISBN 0899424023

The Liturgy of the Hours: Ordinary Time Weeks 1 to 17, Catholic Book Publishing Company, 1980. ISBN 0899424031

The Liturgy of the Hours: Ordinary Time Weeks 18 to 36, Catholic Book Publishing Company, 1980. ISBN 089942404X

Shorter Morning and Evening Prayer, John Brook, Liturgical Press, 1994, 562 pages. ISBN 0814619398

Shorter Christian Prayer, Hard Cover, Catholic Book Publishing Company, 1999. ISBN 0899424082. Leather Cover, ISBN 0899424236

Related Books

The Adoremus Hymnal, Ignatius Press, 1997. Various editions.

The Art of Praying, Msgr. Romano Guardini, Sophia Institute Press, 1995, 192 pages. ISBN 0918477344

Cantors, Cambridge University Press, 1979. ISBN 0521221498

Catechism of the Catholic Church, 2nd edition, Hardcover, Our Sunday Visitor, 2000, 928 pages. ISBN 0879739770. Softcover, ISBN 0879739762

From Breviary to Liturgy of the Hours: The Structural Reform of the Roman Office 1964-1971, Stanislaus Campbell, Pueblo Publishing Company, 1995, 384 pages. ISBN 0814661335

Hymnal for the Hours, GIA Publications Inc., 1989. ISBN 0941050203

Jubilate Deo, GIA Publications Inc.

Liber Usualis, St. Bonaventure Publications, 1953.

Related Church Documents

Apostolicam Actuositatem
Christifideles Laici
Gaudium et Spes
Sacrosanctum Concilium

Internet Resources

Apostolate of Prayer Web Site: *http://prayer.rosaryshop.com* A variety of resources and links for the Liturgy of the Hours, including a Liturgy of the Hours calendar and a chant tutorial CD.

Liturgy of the Hours Web Site: *http://www.liturgyhours.org/* Daily distributes The Liturgy of the Hours in Adobe Portable Document Format (PDF).

Magnificat Web Site: *http://www.magnificat.net/* Monthly periodical with Mass readings and adapted Morning and Evening Prayers.

Universalis Web Site: *http://www.universalis.com/* Daily readings from The Liturgy of the Hours.

Other Resources

St. Thomas More House of Prayer: *http://www.liturgyofthehours.org* Retreat house dedicated to teach the Liturgy of the Hours.

Glossary

Breviary: One of several names for the prayer book used for the Liturgy of the Hours. From the Latin, *breviarium*, "summary."

Canticle: A song taken from the Bible. From the Latin, *canticulum*, "little song."

Common: A collection of readings and prayers shared "in common" by multiple feast days and memorials, such as the Common of Martyrs, from which prayers may be selected on the feast day of any saint who was martyred.

Office: A worship service. From the Latin, *officium*, "service, duty."

Opus Dei: Latin, "The work of God." This is the term St. Benedict uses in his monastic rule for the Liturgy of the Hours.

Ordinary: The parts of the Liturgy of the Hours that do not vary from day to day. From the Latin, *ordinarius*, "usual, customary."

Proper: Parts of the Liturgy of the Hours that vary according to specific day or season. From the Latin, *proprium*, "special, particular."

Psalmody: Refers to methods of sung prayer, particularly the Psalms. The two most common forms of Psalmody are "antiphonal" and "responsorial." Psalmody is antiphonal when halves of the group alternate verses. Psalmody is responsorial when a leader alternates verses with the entire group.

Psalter: The collection of Psalms, canticles, hymns and antiphons used in the Liturgy of the Hours. From the Latin, *psalterium*, "a collection of Psalms." The modern Psalter presents the entire collection of 150 Psalms in a four-week-cycle.

Traditional Names for the Divine Office

The complete Liturgy of the Hours has varied in form throughout Christian history and between communities. A common model has been a series of seven services, or "hours," prayed by religious throughout the day. This arrangement is still customary among some contemplative orders. Acording to the "General Instruction of the Liturgy of the Hours," if a Daytime prayer is used at all, it may consist of one prayer, rather than the three traditional sessions — terce, sext and none. Editions of the Liturgy of the Hours, as well as *Lord, Open My Lips*, are arranged to suit this approach. See the "General Instruction," chapter II, section V, for additional information.

Please note that the times and titles given below represent one of many possible arrangements. Contemporary practice varies widely.

Matins: The Office of Readings. Traditionally prayed very early, 4:00AM, or immediately before Lauds. From the Latin, "morning." Also called "Vigils" (Latin, "awake; alert")

Lauds: Morning Prayer. Traditionally prayed at the beginning of the work day, 6:00AM. From the Latin, "praise."

Terce: Midmorning Prayer. Traditionally prayed at the "third hour," 9:00AM. From the Latin, "third."

Sext: MiddayPrayer. Traditionally prayed at the "sixth hour," 12:00PM. From the Latin, "sixth."

None: Midafternoon Prayer. Traditionally prayed at the "ninth hour," 3:00PM. From the Latin, "ninth."

Vespers: Evening Prayer. Traditionally prayed at the conclusion of the work day, 6:00PM. From the Latin, "evening."

Compline: Night Prayer. The last prayer of the day, 9:00PM. From the Latin, "completion."

About the Author

A former Assistant Director for Ministry Formation for the Archdiocese of Portland, Oregon, Seth Murray holds a Masters Degree in Theological Studies from the University of Dallas Institute for Religious and Pastoral Studies (now headquartered at Ave Maria University in Naples, Florida).

Raised in various Protestant denominations, Seth turned in his Church of the Nazarene local minister license in 1994 and, with his wife, Tyra, entered into full communion with the Catholic Church. He and Tyra own and operate the online store and prayer resource, The Rosary Shop (*http://www.rosaryshop.com/*). They live with their four children in McMinnville, Oregon.